# of HUMAN BEINGS & SIN

NGIM
**Guide to**
**Bible Doctrine**

The
Doctrine
of

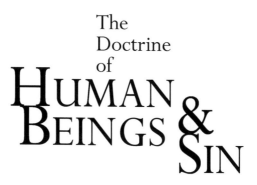

HUMAN
BEINGS &
SIN

Norman L. Geisler
Douglas E. Potter

NGIM
Indian Trail, North Carolina

*The Doctrine of Human Beings & Sin*
*NGIM Guide to Bible Doctrine, Volume 6*
Norman L. Geisler and Douglas E. Potter

Published by Norm Geisler International Ministries | P.O. Box 2638 | Indian Trail,
NC 28079 | USA
www.ngim.org

Printed in the United States of America

ISBN–13: 978-1973837022
ISBN–10: 1973837021

# Contents

**Norm Geisler International Ministries
Guide to Bible Doctrine**

**www.NGIM.org**

# Introduction

Central to the Bible's teaching is that humans are a special creation of God (Gen. 2:7); baring the image of God (Gen. 1:26), yet because of the Fall all of us have a sinful nature (Gen. 2:7; 3:11–12). Understanding the nature of human beings, their sinful condition and its ultimate defeat is important to the Christian faith.

Long technical treaties on this doctrine while important, can be intimidating to the Christian that wants to dig into the study for the first time. Even some less technical approaches might not state the doctrine in as systematic or comprehensive manner as it should. As a result, those new to the study of this doctrine may never be exposed to important concepts and issues.

Christians, more than ever, need a study of humans and sin that is true and systematic. Many in and outside the church do not understand how this doctrine is formulated, how it intersects and informs many areas of Christian thought and life which serves as a foundation to a Christian worldview.

This book is a popular introduction to the study of human beings (Anthropology) and sin (Hamartiology) firmly rooted in the evangelical tradition. Each chapter covers an area of the doctrine, stresses its basis, doctrinal importance and interconnectedness to formulating a Christian view of Humans Beings, Sin and other doctrines. The study questions provided help reinforce the material and make it usable even for a formal study of the doctrine. It is ideal for personal study or in groups for the home, church, school or ministry environment.

The approach is faithful to the historical evangelical position that integrates all truth as God's truth and upholds the classical view of the full inspiration and inerrancy of the Bible.

Dr. Norman L. Geisler has taught theology and Bible doctrine in churches, colleges, and seminaries for over 60 years. Having authored over one hundred works in Christian apologetics and theology (see *Systematic Theology In One Volume*), this work, while maintaining the precision and comprehensiveness the study needs, uniquely makes it accessible to everyone.

Dr. Douglas E. Potter is an assistant professor and Director of the Doctor of Ministry program at Southern Evangelical Seminary. He has been teaching Christian theology and apologetics for over a decade and is an author or co–author of several books.

# 1

## The Origin of Human Beings

*Behold, I was brought forth in iniquity, And in sin my*
*mother conceived me.*
*Psalm 51:5*

God created human beings who are ranked below the angels but above non–rational animals and inanimate matter since man bares the image of God. This chapter as well as the next constitutes our study of human beings (Anthropology). this chapter, investigates the biblical origin and nature of humankind. This is followed by a study of human nature (Chapter 2).

God is absolutely perfect. Only perfection can come from an absolutely perfect being. Deuteronomy 32:4 says, "His [God] work is perfect." Second Samuel 22:31 says, "As for God, his way is blameless [perfect]" and Matthew 5:48: "Your heavenly Father is perfect."

## State of Innocence and Perfection

Man was originally created in a virtuous state (Eccl. 7:29). This entails that his nature was morally perfect, with no knowledge of evil (Gen. 3:5). Such a state was either supernaturally caused or naturally caused by God. Jonathan Edwards (1703–1758) and Thomas Aquinas (1224/5–1274) held that the original state was a super-naturally created state of grace that Adam had before the fall and was lost by his sin. William G. T. Shedd (1820–1894) argued that this created state of perfection was natural, that is the very created nature God gave Adam. Regardless of how it was maintained by God, both views agree that God is perfect and the state of Adam and Eve from the moment of Creation, must have been perfect.

Since God is absolutely perfect, the environment He created for human existence was "very good" (Gen. 1:31). This entails that it was materially and morally perfect. Creation was not subject to corruption as it was after the fall, Romans 8:22 says, "For we know that the whole creation groans and suffers the pains of childbirth together until now." There was no human death. Romans 5:12 says, "Therefore, just as through one man sin entered into the world, and death through sin, and so death spread to all men, because all sinned." The first humans were created with no evil in their natures, they were complete and innocent of any sin; they "did not know good and evil" (Gen. 1, 2). They were morally perfect; this is not simply the lack of vice, but the reality of virtue since "God made men upright." (Eccl. 7:29).

In their original state humankind was not a servant of nature, but a master over it. Genesis 1:28 says, "Fill the earth and subdue it. Rule over the fish of the sea and the birds of the air and over every living creature that moves on the ground." They were morally accountable to God: "the Lord God commanded the man, 'You are free to eat from any tree in the garden; but you must not eat from the tree of the knowledge of good and evil, for when you eat of it you will surely die'" (Gen. 2:16–17). Adam had moral accountability to God.

Adam was free in the sense of his moral actions were self–determined. No one else, including Satan (the Serpent), made Adam and Eve commit sin. These perfect persons in a perfect paradise were not without an imperfect intruder. Satan, a fallen angel of God (Rev. 12:4) led Eve, and through her Adam into disobedience against God (Rom. 5:19; 1 Tim. 2:14). Adam and Eve were not enticed to lie, cheat, steal or curse. They were not vulnerable to these temptations since they were morally perfect. The command God gave them was not a command to stay away from intrinsic evil. Instead, their only vulnerability or test they could undergo was to whether or not they would obey God, because He said it.

Their moral responsibility to God was with regard to an object that was morally neutral. God could have said, for instance, "Don't pick the daisies." The issue was not that the sin was inherent in the substance in which they partook; the temptation to sin was in the enticement to defy God, and subsequently to be conscious of the evil of choosing against Him. *No evil from within or from without drew them to their transgression.* Only a raw act of freedom, wrongly exercised, carried out their disobedience and sealed their doom.

Some have asked, could Adam and Eve committed some other sin before eating the forbidden fruit? The answer may very well be that it was impossible for them to sin on another issue, since they were created morally perfect. Indeed, if there were then Satan would have so tempted them, but there is no indication that he did. Most likely, only disobedience to God's specific command would precipitate the Fall and plunge the whole creation into death and disaster (Rom. 5:12; 1 Tim. 2:14).

## ORIGIN OF THE HUMAN SOUL

There are three views of the origin of the human soul: 1) Preexistence, 2) Creation and 3) the Traducian view. The Preexistence view says the soul existed before creation. The Creation view says the soul is specially created by God when the person comes to be. The Traducian view says the soul is instrumentally caused to exist through the parents when the person comes to be.

The non–Christian understanding of the Preexistence view sees the soul as never being created; instead it exists eternally as a form. This was the Platonic view, from the Greek philosopher Plato. Some early Christians adopted this view but added that it was created from eternity by God. Origen (c. 185–254 A.D.) and the early writings of Augustine (354–430 A.D.) hold this view. However, neither view finds support in Scripture, which clearly teaches the creation, hence the beginning of a soul/body. Human beings have a beginning (Gen. 1:27) and the Bible declares the soul and body are created (Gen. 2:7). Human life begins at conception (see Appendix) and no human (temporal) being can be eternal (uncreated).

The creationist view says God directly creates a new individual soul for everyone born into this world and leaves just the body to be generated by the parents. Some biblical texts are cited for this: Psalm 51:5 says, "Behold, I was brought forth in iniquity, and in sin my mother conceived me." And Matthew 1:20 says, "For the Child who has been conceived in her is of the Holy Spirit." This view also acknowledges that all genetic information is present at conception. Not all creationists agree on when God implants the newly created soul. Some say it is at the moment of conception, others at implantation and others hold it is after implantation. Thomas Aquinas held that an animal soul was generated by the parents, and then God created a rational human soul at animation (movement in mother's womb). Other more extreme views have said creation is at birth or even at first breath (see Appendix).

One serious problem with the creationist view, no matter when it takes place, is that it must attribute the direct creation of each sin nature to God (Ps. 51:5) to account for inherited sin (Chapter 4). Yet this is impossible since God cannot create sin or any sinful substance. Scripture says God has ceased creating after the sixth day of creation (Gen. 2:3). Aquinas' view suffers from an outdated view of biology and science. Aquinas himself held that the body exists for the sake of the soul, and if the body has distinct human only features, such as a complete genetic code at conception that forms the basis of developing human organs, a human rational soul must be present to direct all these human only features. Furthermore, developmental changes in the soul do not make it a different entity or nature, only more mature. The creation of a soul at birth or breath is only the observing of life, not the beginning of life (Gen. 5:1ff). Animals have breath, but are not human and human life exists even when there is no breathing (Phil. 1:23). Hence, Scripture speaks of full human life in the womb at conception (Ps. 51:5; Matt. 1:20). In short, the creationist view does not explain the inheritance of original sin.

The term "Traducian" comes from the Latin *tradux* which means "branch of a vine." This view says each new human being is a branch of the parents. Both soul and body are naturally generated together by the father and mother. This must be the case because God's creation was completed on the sixth day (Gen. 2:2) and He is now resting (Heb. 4:4). Scientifically it says once the sperm and ovum of the parents are conceived in the womb a full individual human person exists. There is a good deal of biblical support for this view.

The biblical basis for the Traducian view is found throughout Scripture. The creation of Adam's soul by God is a special case since he was the first human and was perfect. But Eve was made from Adam, and not separately (Gen. 2:21–22). This shows the unity of male and female since the female is made from the male (1 Cor. 11:8). Eve is called the "mother of all the living" (Gen. 3:20) and Adam had children in his image (Gen. 5:3). This only makes sense if full human life is transmitted by natural generation. The term "flesh" as used in Scripture can mean the "whole person with body" rather than just their physical body (John 3:6; Rom. 1:3; 3:20). Furthermore, God's offspring, who bare His image are "one blood" and this was accomplished by natural processes (Acts 17:26). Levi was in Abraham's loins which implies physical transmission (Heb. 7:10). The human body in the womb is a full human person (Ps. 22:9–10; Jer. 1:5). This also accounts for how all sinned through one man (Rom. 5:12) which implies sin can be transmitted by natural processes. We are born with a sinful nature (Eph. 2:3) which makes no sense if it is just the body without the soul since bodies without souls cannot sin. We are conceived in sin (Ps. 51:5) which is something not possible unless a soul is present. Finally, Jesus, is from the "loins" of David indicating a genetic connection (1 Kings 8:19). All this indicates that the biblical view is that the personal substance is more than physical and, since God has rested from creating (Gen. 2:1–3; Heb. 4:4), the soul was made instrumentally in the womb by a natural process.

In addition to the biblical support, there are other reasons to favor the Traducian view. This view accounts for the imputation of sin from Adam to the entire posterity which must be by natural processes. Romans 5:18 says, "So then as through one transgression there resulted condemnation to all men, even so through one act of righteousness there resulted justification of life to all men." Life or the soul begins at conception. This helps explain the universal natural inclination to sin (Eph. 2:3; John 3:6) that favors the Traducian view. Also, the soul/body unity view, which is defended below, favors the Traducian view, since both are transmitted from parent to child. Scientifically human DNA is naturally passed on from parent to child. Hence, biologically everything is present at conception to constitute a human person. This is also supported by analogy with the animal world; non-rational animal souls likewise are passed on from parents to offspring. Hence, humans are a psychosomatic, soul/body unity. The physical body is not the whole person and neither is the immaterial soul, but together they constitute a complete human being.

Some have objected to this view saying Hebrews 12:9, calls God the "Father of our spirits." However, it does not say He created our spirit at conception. Even if fathering is creation, it does not say how it was done. Fathering may be indicative of care related to His disciplining us.

Others have objected that Isaiah 57:16 says, "The breath of man [soul] that I have created." Here it should be noted that the Traducian view acknowledges that God is the efficient cause of the human soul, but not the secondary instrumental cause. Also "soul" in Scripture is often used of the whole person, body and soul. And the term "created" could be understood as "made" that does not usually entail "creation from nothing." Furthermore, this text does not indicate how or when. Hence, with these considerations in mind, a Traducian understanding is still possible.

Still others have objected to the traducian view saying that only God can create and all creation is dependent on God's necessity. Hence, parents cannot be the cause of their children's soul. However, the traducian view does not hold the parents are the *efficient* cause of their children's existence. They are only the *instrumental* cause. Parents cause the *becoming* of their child; God alone causes the *being* of the child. The question is not about the origin and sustenance of a human soul, which only God can do, but the transmission of the soul, which the parents facilitate.

In short, the Traducian view correctly acknowledges that all creation depends upon God's necessity. It does not deny the efficient cause of God, only the instrumental cause. The parents cause the becoming of their child, only God can cause their being (existence) and the parents do pass on the soul–body unity, which only God did and can create and sustain.

The following table (1.1) summarizes the three views of the origin of the soul.

| | Pre–Existence | Creationism | Traducianism |
|---|---|---|---|
| TIME OF CREATION | From Eternity (Plato) Before World (Origen) | 1) At Conception, 2) Or Implantation 3) At Animation, or 4) At Birth | Originally in Adam Instrumentally through parents |
| GOD'S ROLE | Created all souls | Creates each soul | Creates body and soul through parents |
| PARENT'S ROLE | Soul: none Body: Efficient cause | Soul: Occasional cause Body: Efficient cause | Body and Soul: Instrumental cause |
| NATURE OF MAN | Man *is* a soul (Man *has* a body) | Man *is* a soul (Man *has* a body) | Man is soul–body unity |
| IMAGE OF GOD | In soul only | In soul only | In soul and body* |
| IMMORTALITY | Soul only | Soul only | Soul and body |

*Not all Traducians hold this view.

Table 1.1

## SUMMARY

God created everything perfect. This perfection included free will which made evil possible. God created Adam a perfect unity of body and soul. Of the views that dispute how individual souls come into being after Adam, it appears the traducian view, as opposed to the pre–existent or direct creation view, better fits all the biblical and scientific data. Only the traducian view adequately accounts for the fallen soul being generated at conceptions by the parents as opposed to a direct cause by God.

**Questions to Answer**
1. What is the biblical support for creation originally being made perfect?
2. How could Adam and Eve be tempted if they were innocent and perfect?
3. What are the three main views regarding the origin of the soul?
4. What biblical verses support the Traducian view of the soul?

# 2

## The Nature of Human Beings

*Then the LORD God formed man of dust from the ground,*
*and breathed into his nostrils the breath of life; and man*
*became a living being.*
*Genesis 2:7*

This chapter explores the nature of human beings, the image of God in man, free will and the soul–body relationship as taught in the Bible. Humans are created in the image of God. Genesis 1:27 says, "And God created man in His own image, in the image of God He created him; male and female He created them" (cf. Gen. 5:1). First Corinthians 11:7 says, "For a man . . . is the image and glory of God" and Colossians 3:10 says of believers that we "have put on the new self who is being renewed to a true knowledge according to the image of the One who created him."

### THE IMAGE OF GOD IN MAN

The meaning of this image and likeness entails that man resembles God in several ways. It includes an intellectual *resemblance* to God. God alone is all knowing, but humans have intelligence and will (Col. 3:10; Jude 10). It includes a moral likeness to God. God is love, but humans can love (1 John 4:16). God can create, but human beings can *reproduce* and make (Gen. 1:28). Humans *represent* God on earth (Gen. 1:28) and humans are morally *responsible* to God; able to choose right from wrong (Gen. 2:16–17). Also, the image of God is evident in the reasons humans should not be harmed or cursed, since it is wrong to murder or curse humans. Genesis 9:6 says, "Whoever sheds man's blood, by man his blood shall be shed, for in the image of God He made man." And James 3:9 says, "With it [tongue] we bless our Lord and Father; and with it we curse men, who have been made in the likeness of God."

Furthermore, the image of God not only applies to the immaterial aspect of humans, the soul, but also includes the body which emphasizes the soul/body unity that constitutes the whole person. This understanding is strongly supported in Scripture. God created matter good which constitutes the body (Gen. 1:31). He created humans male and female which entails their bodies are in the image of God (Gen. 1:27). The basis for murder being wrong is that it includes God's image in the body which humans can kill not the soul alone which cannot be killed (Gen. 9:6). Christ incarnate, in bodily form is the image of God according to Hebrews 1:3 that says, "And He [Jesus Christ] is the radiance of His glory and the exact representation of His nature." Also, the fact that there is a resurrection of the body shows it is part of the whole person that is in God's image.

But man, in the image of God does not entail God in the image of man. This teaching does not imply God

has a body; any more than the "word" I write with material ink on material paper means the thought in my
mind must also be material, as it is on the ink and paper.
Furthermore, angels are like God since they are immaterial, but God is not like them in the sense of being created
and finite.

Also of importance is that fallen man is still in God's
image (Gen. 9:6; 1 Cor. 11:7; James 3:9). Even the most
vile of human beings retain God's likeness, be it oh so vi-
tiated by sin. And redeemed humans are being renewed
after God's image. Ephesians 4:24 says, "And put on the
new self, which in the likeness of God has been created
in righteousness and holiness of the truth." And 1 John
3:2 says, "Beloved, now we are children of God, and it
has not appeared as yet what we shall be. We know that,
when He appears, we shall be like Him, because we shall
see Him just as He is" (cf. Rom. 8:29; 2 Cor. 3:18; Col.
3:10).

The image of God in humans entails several areas of
moral responsibility. Man is responsible for himself (Eph.
5:28, 29), for the world (Gen. 1:28), to fellow man (Gen.
4:9; 9:6; Acts 17:26) and ultimately to God (Gen. 2:16,
17). Such responsibility entails and should point us to-
wards our intended ultimate end which is to see God, our
creator, face to face. (1 John 3:2; Rev. 22:4).

## HUMAN FREE WILL

An important aspect of the image of God (Gen. 1:27) in
man is his free will. Man was created with free will, the
power to choose good or evil. This is implied in the commands of God toward man (Gen. 1:28; 2:16, 17). Such
responsibility implies that man has the ability to freely
respond. This is also clearly entailed in the command to

love (Matt. 22:37). Love can be commanded but not demanded. Forced love is a contradiction. Man exercised his own free will to sin and fallen man is willfully rebellious to God (Rom. 1:18; Eph. 2:2). It is true that fallen man cannot of his own sinful will be saved (John 1:13). But man is free with respect to so–called "horizontal" matters and even some "vertical" matters. With respect to horizontal matters he is free to choosing a mate (1 Cor. 7:39), make family decisions (1 Cor. 7:37), decisions within the church (1 Peter 5:2), the giving of money (2 Cor. 9:7) and making requests to friends (Philemon 14).

While humans are not free to initiate or attain their own salvation, they are free to accept God's free gift of salvation (Matt. 23:37; 2 Peter 3:9). We can accept God's revelation of salvation: since it is the "gift" of salvation that must be "received." John 1:12 says, "But as many as received Him, to them He gave the right to become children of God, even to those who believe in His name" (cf. Rom. 6:23). Even the Old Testament recognized that a new heart from God is "given" (Ezek. 11:19). God expects us to "choose" Him (Deut. 30:15; Josh. 24:14; 1 Kings 18:21).

Human free will is the God given power of moral and spiritual self–determinism. That is the ability to do otherwise. Freedom is doing what one *decides*, not what one *desires*. One can decide contrary to their desires. This is entailed by God holding us responsible for our decisions. Responsibility implies the ability to respond. Determinism is ultimately self–defeating since according to determinism non–determinists should accept their view; "ought" implies free to change but according to the determinists view they are determined not to hold it. Since such a view takes away free choose from a person, they are no longer persons. It reduces a person to an object: turns an "I" into an "it." Furthermore, praise and blame become meaningless if we are not free and even God's commands would be meaningless. Nonsense or humor also is only possible if someone can willfully violate the rules of language. For objections to free will that come from man's sinful condition see Chapter 3.

## BODY/SOUL RELATIONSHIP

The Bible uses several terms to designate the immaterial or spiritual dimension of humans. The term *soul* sometimes actually includes the body. This is evident in Genesis 2:7 which says, "Then the LORD God formed man of dust from the ground, and breathed into his nostrils the breath of life; and man became a living being." And Psalm 16:10 says, "For You will not abandon my *soul* to Sheol (Grave); nor will you allow Your Holy One to undergo decay." Sometimes it is used to distinguish the soul from the body (Gen. 35:18). *Spirit* is almost always used for the immaterial dimension of humans and is sometimes used interchangeable with *soul* (Luke 1:46, 24:38–39; James 2:26; John 19:30, 4:24). The term *heart* is used for the whole inner person and includes the mind (Rom. 10:9; Deut. 6:5; Matt. 12:34). The term *mind* is used for the inner dimension that thinks and imagines (Mark 12:30; 12:2; Rom. 8:6–7, 12:2; 2 Cor. 10:5).

Likewise, there are terms used for the material dimension of humans. *Body* is used for the material aspect of humans (Matt. 10:28; James 2:26; 1 Cor. 15:42–44, 53) and *flesh* is used for the physical dimension (Luke 24:39; Acts 2:31). Some phrases are also used, "flesh and blood" (Matt. 16:17; 1 Cor. 15:50) emphasizes the mortal aspect of humans. Analogies are also found in Scripture, especially by Paul who uses "earthen vessel" (2 Cor. 4:7), "earthly tent" (2 Cor. 5:1; John 1:14) and "outward man" (2 Cor. 4:16).

Philosophically there are six views of the soul–body relationship (see Table 2.1). 1) Materialism says only the body exists; there is no soul (Thomas Hobbes 1588–1679). 2) Idealism says only the soul exists; there is no body (George Berkeley 1685–1753). 3) Monism says the soul and body are two sides, inner and outer, of one substance or the same thing (Benedict Spinoza 1632–1677). 4) Dualism (Dichotomy) says the soul and body are two separate substances or parallel entities that never intersect (attributed to Plato c. 427–347 B.C. and René Descartes 1596–1650). 5) Trichotomy says there is body,

| View of Soul/Body | Description | Proponent |
|---|---|---|
| Materialism | Only the body exists | Thomas Hobbes 1588–1679 |
| Idealism | Only the soul exists | George Berkeley 1685–1753 |
| Monism | Soul and body are two sides, inner and outer, of one substance | Benedict Spinoza 1632–1677 |
| Dualism (Dichotomy) | Soul and body are two separate substances or parallel entities that never intersect | Plato c. 427–347 B.C. René Descartes 1596–1650 |
| Trichotomy | Body, soul, and spirit | Plotinus 205–270 B.C. Tertullian c. 155–225 A.D. |
| Hylomorphism | Soul/body unity | Aristotle 384–322 B.C. Thomas Aquinas 1224/5–1274 |

Table 2.1

soul, and spirit (origins in Plato, Plotinus 205–270 B.C. and Tertullian c. 155–225 A.D. adopted it). And finally, 6) Hylomorphism says humans are a soul/body unity. The roots of Hylomorphism are in the Old Testament, found philosophically in Aristotle (384–322 B.C.) and corroborated by Thomas Aquinas (1224/5–1274).

Materialism cannot be supported by Scripture since the body and soul exist and are distinguishable. The body will perish, not the soul (2 Cor. 4:16; 5:1; Gen. 35:18). This view is self–defeating since the materialistic view or concept is not made up of matter. There must be a transcendent "I" to even account for the existence of the view. Also, the universe has a non–material origin "out of nothing" (Chapter 4). Hence, Mind produced matter, not the reverse, matter producing mind. Furthermore, there are other immaterial things; for example, the moral law is not material, since it is prescriptive (not descriptive), and there must be a principle of life that distinguishes living things from nonliving things. Hence, materialism that there is only a body or matter cannot be true.

Idealism also is not supported in Scripture since God created a material universe (Gen. 1) and God is Spirit (John 4:26). Matter is finite and destructible (1 Cor. 15:42), yet God is not (1 Tim. 6:16). The soul and body are different since they are separated at death (Luke 24:30; John 2:26) and Scripture argues for the resurrection of the "body." Yet, if there is no material body, why should there need to be a resurrection to constitute the person? This view begs the question, since it assumes only minds exist. It assumes ideas are the only formal objects of knowing. Yet this is contrary to experience since we know that there is a difference between eating real food verses thinking (an idea) about eating food. Finally, this view charges God with deception. God may be all powerful to create a world of just ideas, but He is also all good and cannot deceive us making us think it is other than what it is. Hence idealism, that there is only a soul and no body or matter, cannot be true.

Monism, that soul and body are one substance, is not supported either since it denies the two dimensions (soul/body) that the Bible affirms. Such a view cannot explain how the soul survives death which the Bible affirms. Further, it cannot explain how Jesus is alive between death and resurrection (Luke 24:46; John 19:30). Such a view must entail annihilationism and immediate resurrection at death. Yet the Bible denies both of these. This view also assumes an identical understanding of the body and soul. Such a position is contrary to consciousness and thoughts that are clearly different from and not dependent upon the body or matter. Hence Monism, that there is only one substance to constitute a human, cannot be true.

Dualism says the soul and body are two separate substances or parallel entities that never intersect. However, this view denies the biblical teaching of unity (see Hylomorphism below). It also suffers from the problem of having no way for the immaterial soul to know the material world. Actually, it has no way for the soul to even know its own body. Some have postulated a third medium to connect the soul to a body so it can know the world and itself. However, this just complicates matters. What is that third medium made out of, soul or matter? It also entails humans are essentially immaterial. That is a soul using a body as a sailor uses a ship. But this leads to asceticism since human essence is then just spiritual. That is, a human person is a soul and has a body. Hence, this view cannot be true either.

Trichotomy says that humans are composed of body, soul, and spirit. Usually the body is identified with world-consciousness, the soul is identified with self-conscious, and the spirit with God conscious. This has been argued for from Scripture, for example, Hebrews 4:12 says soul and spirit are divided. However, this is a figure of speech describing the power of the Word of God that is able to divide the indivisible and not a reference to the nature of humans. They point to 1 Thessalonians 5:23 that list all three, "spirit and soul and body" separately. But this could also be a way of stressing wholeness and lists both "soul and spirit" to emphasize completeness. They point to Romans 8:16 that speaks of spirit being connected with God; but there are counter examples of the soul being connected to God (Matt. 22:37; Luke 1:46). Some have also pointed to Mark 10:45 saying that Jesus gives his life [soul], not spirit. But if so, then John 19:30 says He gave up His spirit. So, if the Trichotomist view is true, Jesus would not be fully human.

Ultimately the problem with this view is that it is trying to force a Platonic view, that the soul alone is the person which just has a body, into Scripture. Some Christians have adopted this view seeing that it portrays a Trinity in man. However, it is inconsistent, since the same linguistic use applies to "heart" and "mind" which would make man not three parts but five parts. And of most importance is that it follows an incorrect view of language in its interpretation of Scripture. That is, it thinks meaning is absolute because words must correspond to things in the world in a fixed one-to-one relationship. However, words have a one-to-many relationship. That is, the same word can describe multiply things and still show meaning is absolute.

The preceding views are unable to support the biblical data and correct understanding since they do not acknowledge the immaterial dimension (Materialism), the material dimension (Idealism), the possibility of separation (Monism) or material/immaterial interaction (Dualism), or the correct biblical grammatical use of terms (Trichotomy). Only the view of anthropological Hylomorphism, which finds its roots in the Old Testament, expresses humanity as a soul/body unity (not an identity) which can explain the biblical data and correct understanding. The difference between the Platonic and Christian view of human nature is clearly seen in Table 2.2 which is adapted from George Ladd, *The Pattern of New Testament Truth*, Eerdmans, 1977.

Creation involves a unity of dust (matter) and breath (soul) as described in Genesis 2:7. Also, as we have shown soul can mean person and includes the body (Ps. 16:10 cf. Acts 2:30–31) and the soul can be used of a dead body (Lev. 19:28; 21:1). Also, if humans are not a unity, then murder of a body would not be wrong. But Genesis 9:6 clearly indicates it is wrong because it is an attack on the image of God that includes the body. Paul says in 2 Corinthians 5:1–4 that the soul without a body is naked. This imagery is not possible without a unity. Furthermore, the resurrection is supernatural and makes no sense if we are complete without a body.

Such a view also allows for a knowing intellect since they function as a unit. This is easily seen through psychological interaction since together they constitute one substance. The soul influences the body and vice versa. Upon hearing sad news, the emotion of grief affects not

| Platonic view of Human Nature | Christian View of Human Nature |
|---|---|
| Dualistic | Unity |
| Is a Soul (Soul is complete without body) | Is a Soul/Body (Soul is not complete without body) |
| Matter is not good | Matter is good |
| Reincarnation into another body | Resurrection in the same body |
| Body is prison/tomb | Body is expression of the soul |
| Body is the enemy of soul | Body is the friend of soul |
| Soul is simple | Soul is composed |
| Soul is indestructible | Soul is destructible |
| Salvation from the body | Salvation in the body |
| Salvation is by knowledge | Salvation is by faith |
| Soul is divine | Soul is human |
| Soul is eternal | Soul had a beginning |
| Soul preexisted | Soul was created |
| Earth is an alien place | Earth is a friendly place |
| Humans have three parts (body, soul, and spirit) | Humans have two dimensions (inner and outer) |
| Sin results from body burdening soul | Sin results from rebellion of will |
| Redemption of soul | Redemption of whole person |
| God is known by fleeing the world | God is known in and through the world |
| Salvation is by human effort | Salvation is by divine visitation |
| Reality is in the invisible realm | Reality includes the visible realm |

Table 2.2

only the soul, but also the body when it cries. Likewise, pain experienced in the body affects the immaterial soul or mind.

One objection raised is how can the soul separate from the body, if both are one? However, we have argued that soul/body is a unity, not an identity. This is not the Monistic understanding. The soul is to the body as thought is to words on paper. Words are a physical expression of thought; but thought remains even when the paper perishes. Unity does not entail that they are inseparable.

Human beings are not robots or androids, they are persons with intellect (mind), emotion (feeling), will (choice), and conscience (moral capacity). The Bible affirms these aspects of humanity. Humans are created with self-reflecting minds that have the power of syllogistic reasoning (Prov. 23:23) which places them above "unreasoning animals" (Jude 10). This enables humans to worship God (Matt. 22:37) and although capable of great evil (Eccl. 7:25) by redemption it can be renewed (Col. 3:10; Rom. 12:2). Humans are capable of deep emotions and feelings, such as joy and sorrow. Unlike animals, humans are created with a moral capacity to know right from wrong and will choose one over the other (Gen. 2:16–17). Humans, unlike any other creature on earth, have a God-given conscience. Even in our fallen state, God holds us responsible for avoiding evil (Rom. 2:12–15). Although our fallen conscience is fallible, it reflects an innate capacity to know right from wrong, even though it can be distorted (Rom. 2:15) and even "seared" by intense evil (1 Tim. 4:2). However, there is a moral law even though our fallen understanding of it is obscured by sin. It is prescriptive, perfect (Ps. 19:7) objective, and universal

(Rom. 2:15). Indeed, humans have other capacities such as laughter (risibility), the ability to create and enjoy music, art and appreciate beauty which all flows from rationality and part of our human nature.

## SUMMARY

The study of human nature shows that the first human couple was created by God in a perfect state in the image of God. Hence, we resemble God in terms of an intellectual and moral likeness. This image also entails human free choice which is still operative after the fall. While God is the efficient cause of the human soul, it is instrumentally generated through the parents. This best accounts for the transmission of sin. It is also in agreement with the understanding of humans as a soul/body unity that constitutes the whole person.

### Questions to Answer

1. What is the significance and meaning of humans being made in the "image of God?"
2. What biblical support is there for the presence of human free will after the fall?
3. What are the main views regarding the body/soul relationship?
4. What biblical support is there for the understanding of the soul/body unity?

# 3

## The Origin & Nature of Sin

*There is none righteous, not even one; there is none who*
*understands, there is none who seeks for God; all have*
*turned aside, together they have become useless; there is*
*none who does good, there is not even one.*
*Romans 3:10–12*

Although God created the first human couple perfect and set them in a perfect environment (Chapter 1), they disobeyed the word of God and fell into sin. This chapter begins the study of sin (Hamartiology) which covers the origin and nature of sin. The next chapters cover the effects (Chapter 4) and defeat (Chapter 5) of sin.

Because of God's perfect nature (Matt. 5:48), He cannot sin or produce sin (Gen. 1:31). He cannot do evil (Heb. 6:18; Titus 1:2). He cannot tempt anyone (James 1:13), and He cannot approve of sin (Hab. 1:13). While God cannot produce or approve of sin, He can and does permit sin.

## Permission of Sin (by God)

God is the standard of all perfection. Matthew 5:48 says, "Your heavenly Father is perfect." As we have seen, a flawless Being cannot act in a flawed way. Genesis 1:31 says, "God saw all that He had made, and behold, it was very good." God did not create evil (Gen. 3:1f.; 1 Tim. 3:6). Instead, human and angelic creatures introduced sin into God's creation and therefore fell into condemnation.

It is also true that God cannot do evil (Heb. 6:18). Titus 1:2 says, "God, who cannot lie, . . ." and God cannot tempt any one to do evil. James 1:13 says, "God cannot be tempted by evil, and He Himself does not tempt any." God also cannot look on sin with approval. Habakkuk 1:13 says, "Your eyes are too pure to approve evil, And You cannot look on wickedness with favor."

However, God can permit sin. Permitting sin is not necessarily a sin. The Government permits sin by allowing cars to be driven on the roads. Allowing cars is not evil, even though they can produce evil. God by creating the good of free choice, permitted sin (but freedom is good). Genesis 50:20 says, "As for you, you meant evil against me, but God meant it for good in order to bring about this present result, to preserve many people alive." And Hebrews 12:11 says, "All discipline for the moment seems not to be joyful, but sorrowful; yet to those who have been trained by it, afterwards it yields the peaceful fruit of righteousness." It is also true that God can produce a greater good out of sin. Romans 5:20 says, "Where sin abounded, grace abounded much more" (cf. Rom. 5:3f). Also, James 1:2–4 says, "Consider it all joy, my brethren, when you encounter various trials, knowing that the testing of your faith produces endurance. And let endurance have its perfect result, so that you may be perfect and complete, lacking in nothing."

## ORIGIN OF SIN (BY CREATURES)

As we have seen, God created only good creatures (Gen. 1:31; 1 Tim. 4:4; Ps. 148:2, 5) and sin began in heaven before it did on earth.

### The Origin of Sin in Heaven by Angels

Satan and one–third of the angels sinned or rebelled against God (1 Tim. 3:6; 2 Peter 2:4; Jude 6; Rev. 12:3–4). No doubt, evil was born in the breast of an archangel in the presence of God. Isaiah provides an emulation of the first archangel, who rebelled against God:

> How you have fallen from heaven, O star of the morning, son of the dawn! . . . But you said in your heart, 'I will ascend to heaven; I will raise my throne above the stars of God, and I will sit on the mount of assembly In the recesses of the north. 'I will ascend above the heights of the clouds; I will make myself like the Most High.' (Isa. 14:12–14; cf. 1 Tim. 3:6)

Revelation says other angels, a third of them, rebelled with Satan and became demons.

> Then another sign appeared in heaven: and behold, a great red dragon having seven heads and ten horns, and on his heads were seven diadems. And his tail swept away a third of the stars of heaven and threw them to the earth. . . . And the great dragon was thrown down, the serpent of old who is called the devil and Satan, who deceives the whole world; he was thrown down to the earth, and his angels were thrown down with him. (Rev. 12:3–9)

Sin was in the universe before it was in the world. Sin was in heaven before there was sin on earth. This is evidence by the presence of the tempter (Satan) in the Garden (Gen. 3).

### The Origin of Sin on Earth by Humans

Sin began with the first human couple on earth (Gen. 3). After they sinned their eyes were opened . . . naked . . . covered themselves (Gen. 3:7) and hid from God (8). They blamed each other (12) and the serpent (13). As a result, God pronounced a curse on the serpent, the women and Adam. Creation is cursed because of the man's sin: "Cursed is the ground because of you [man]" (17) and death resulted: now he (man) will return to dust (17). The origin of earthly evil is through human free will.

What is the cause of human sin on earth? To properly answer this question, we must take into account the different kinds of causes. The efficient cause of sin is the person (that *by which* sin came to be). The final cause is pride (that *for which* sin came to be). The formal cause is disobedience (that *of which* sin came to be). The material cause is eating forbidden fruit (that *out of which* sin came to be). The exemplar cause does not exist or is none; since it was the first human sin (that *after which* sin came to be). And the instrumental cause is the human power of free choice (that *through which* sin came to be).

Was Adam determined to sin? There are only three logical possible answers. The first possibility is called Determinism that says all human actions are caused by another (not by one-self). This has two versions, hard and soft. The Hard Determinism says there is no free choice at all. The Soft Determinism says there is free choice, but sees it as controlled by God. The second possibility is Indeterminism that says human actions are not caused by anything. The final possibility is Self-determinism that says human free actions are self-caused (caused by

| | Determinism | Indeterminism | Self–Determinism |
|---|---|---|---|
| Cause | Choices are caused by another | Choices are uncaused | Choices are caused by self |
| Contrary act | Could not do otherwise | Could have been otherwise | Could have been otherwise |
| Previous conditions | Causal | Non–causal | Non–causal |
| Future | Determined (like dominos) | Undetermined (like dice) | Determined by God, free for humankind (like foreseeing an accident) |
| All–knowing Mind | Knows all future acts | Knows all except free acts | Knows all future acts |
| Illustration | Hard determinism: Being carried out (as against one's will) Soft determinism: being forced out (as by a weapon) | Blown out (as by the wind) | Lured out (as by someone else) |
| Model | Puppet | Erratic electron | Free agent |

Table 3.1

one's self). Either Adam's sin was caused by another (determined), uncaused (indetermined), or caused by himself (self–determined). However, it was not determined by God, because God cannot and did not cause Adam to sin. And neither did the tempter (Satan) force him to sin. It also was not Indeterminism, since there is no lack of wholeness in Adam that would give rise to sin (he was perfect) and there are no such things as uncaused actions. Therefore, Adam's sin is self–determined, that is, determined by himself. Adam must have caused it himself. Adam was free in the sense that his act was self–determined (Gen. 2:16). His evil choice was not inevitable (Gen. 2:17). He had the power to obey or disobey and he was held responsible, which implies the ability to respond.

### FURTHER QUESTIONS ABOUT GOD, SIN AND FREE WILL

The origin of sin through Adam and Eve's disobedience raises important questions about human free will. Adam's act involved a decision between good and evil, and it was free in that it could have been avoided. God said Adam "should not" or "ought not" to have sinned (Gen. 2:17). *Ought* implies *can*—what one should do implies that he is able to do it. God held him responsible, even punishing him for choosing wrongly.

If God is sovereignly in control of all things, including human choices, then did God cause Adam to sin? This question assumes an extreme Calvinist claim that free will is simply doing what we *desire*. And no one ever desires to do good unless God gives him the desire to do so. In chapter 2, however, we defined and defended human free will as the God given power of moral and spiritual self–determinism. That is the ability to do otherwise. Freedom is doing what one *decides*, not what one *desires*. One can decide contrary to their desires.

But if the extreme Calvinist view is consistently carried through, then God is responsible for all human actions. It makes God responsible for evil. Put bluntly, this means that when a murder occurs, it is God who is accountable for the death of the victim. This is the logical outworking of determinism. God did not make Adam sin. He did not place the desire in Adam's heart to disobey Him. God is absolutely good and, as such, He cannot do or be responsible for evil. As we have shown, Adam sinned by his own free will, the ability to *decide* to do otherwise. If God made free creatures, and it is good for us to be free, then the origin of evil is in the misuse of freedom.

How can God be free if there is no possibility that He can choose wrongly? The original humans were free to sin or not sin. God is free, yet He cannot sin (Hab. 1:13). God cannot even be tempted to sin (James 1:13). The answer is that God is free in the sense of having the power of self–determination (God is the *efficient* cause of His own choices), but not in the libertarian sense of having the ability to choose to do other than God. God in His very essence is all–goodness and therefore, He can only do good, being in accord with His own Eternal nature.

How can humans be free and yet not be able to sin in heaven? While in the world, human free choice involves self–determination (to be the efficient cause of our own choices) and the ability to do other than good (that is evil). But in heaven we will be in a perfected state, similar to God, in that we will have the self–determined ability to choose only the good. This is not the destruction of true freedom, but the fulfillment of it. In heaven, the freedom to do evil vanishes and we are free to do only the good.

The essence of true freedom is self–determined ability to choose only the good. Likewise, in hell, evil persons without the influence of God's grace, will be solidified in their will to do evil. The loss of the ability to do evil is not an evil of any kind; rather it is a profound good. Heaven is the completion of our freedom, not a negation of it.

## The Nature of Sin

What is a moral wrong? There are many terms used for moral wrong in the Bible. Some of these include *sin* that means "to miss," "to forfeit," or "to lack" (Ps. 51:4), "to miss the mark," "to err," "to sin" (Rom. 3:23). *Trespass* means "to cover up," "to act covertly, treacherously, grievously" (Num. 31:16), "to slip," "to stumble aside," "to offend," or "to sin" (Gal. 6:1). *Iniquity* means "perversity," "fault," "iniquity" (Isa. 53:11), "morally wrong," "unjust," "unrighteous" (James 3:6). *Evil* means "bad," "harmful," "wrong," "calamity" (Isa. 7:15), "evil in effect" (Matt. 7:11), "evil in character" (Rom. 7:21). *Wickedness* means "morally bad" or "ungodly" (Ps. 1:1), (Matt. 23:28; 24:12; Rom. 6:19; 2 Cor. 6:14). *Desire* is also used for evil "strong desire," "passion" or "lust" (Rom. 7:8; Col. 3:5; 1 Thess. 4:5).

There are two basic kinds or categories of sin in the Bible. The first includes sins of commission which is doing what we should not do. First John 3:4 says, "Everyone who sins breaks the law; in fact, sin is lawlessness." The second are sins of omission that is not doing what we should do. James 4:17 says, "Anyone, then, who knows the good he ought to do and doesn't do it, sins." Both kinds of sins, commission and omission, are blame worthiness (Isa. 53:6, cf. Lev. 16:21).

There are seven detestable sins singled out, these are pride, deceit, murder, plotting evil, quickness to do wrong, false testimony, and troublemaking (Prov. 6:16–19). Paul lists over forty different designations or descriptions of sin in Romans 1, these include: godlessness, wickedness, suppress the truth, non–glorifying of God, futile, foolish, exchanging God's glory for an image, sinful desires, sexual impurity, degrading their bodies, lying, worshiping and serving created things, shameful lust, unnatural relations, lust, indecent acts, perversion, rejecting the knowledge of God, depraved mind, doing what ought not to be done, filled with every kind of wickedness, evil, greed, depravity, envy, murder, strife, deceit, malice, gossips, slanderers, god–haters, insolent, arrogant, boastful, doing evil, disobeying parents, senseless, faithless, heartless, and ruthless.

Paul in Galatians 5 lists fifteen different depictions of sin as "works of the flesh" as follows: sexual immorality, impurity, debauchery, idolatry, witchcraft, hatred, discord, jealousy, fits of rage, selfish ambition, dissensions, factions, envy, drunkenness, and orgies. He concludes, "of which I forewarn you, just as I have forewarned you, that those who practice such things will not inherit the kingdom of God" (Gal. 5:21).

Sin as committed against God is described as unbelief, as Paul said, "whatever is not from faith is sin" (Rom. 14:23). Jesus said, "He who believes in Him is not judged; he who does not believe has been judged already, because he has not believed in the name of the only begotten Son of God" (John 3:18, cf. Heb. 11:6). Sin is rebellion against God, since God is King and we are His subjects, we have rebelled against his rule in our lives (Prov. 17:11, Neh. 9:17).

While all sin is offensive to God, not all sins are considered by God to be equal. There are degrees of sin and severity. Jesus said there are "weightier matters of the law" (Matt. 23:23), we have a higher duty in the "first and greatest commandment" (Matt. 22:38) and some are "guilty of a greater sin" (John 19:11). Some sin can even lead to God taking the person's life (1 John 5:16; 1 Cor. 11:29–30). There is also the greatest sin, blasphemy of the Holy Spirit (Matt. 12:32). There are even degrees of eternal punishment for the heaviness or severity of the sins committed (Rev. 20:12).

Sin always has an offender, someone who is offended by the sinner. Proverbs 8:36 says, "But he who sins against me injures himself; All those who hate me love death." Hence, the sinner first offends himself by his own sin. Proverbs 6:32 says, "The one who commits adultery with a woman is lacking sense; He who would destroy himself does it." It is also offence against others and society. First Corinthians 15:33, says "Do not be deceived: 'Bad company corrupts good morals.' "

Humans are so sinful that no comparison exists between them and God (Rom. 3:10–18). Hence, sin is most importantly an offence against heaven or the eternal God (Luke 15:18). Sin is unbelief (Rom. 14:23; John 3:18; Heb. 11:6), sin is rebellion (1 Sam. 15:23; Prov. 17:11; Neh. 9:17), sin is transgression (Rom. 5:14; 1 John 3:4; Ps. 51:4), and sin is pride (1 Tim. 3:6; Ezek. 28:17; 1 John 2:16).

Sin is anything that falls short of God's perfect moral nature. Paul said, "for all have sinned and fall short of the glory of God" (Rom. 3:23, cf. Lev. 11:45). The ultimate objective standard is God's absolute moral perfection, anything that falls short of it is sin. God has six basic mor-

al attributes. God is holiness in that He is totally and ut-
terly set apart from all evil (Lev. 11:44–45). God is justice
in that He is intrinsically the absolute standard of justice
or righteousness (Ps. 89:14; Heb. 1:8). God is perfection
in that He is impeccable, flawless excellence or perfect in
every way (Deut. 34:4; 2 Sam. 22:31). God is jealous to
denote zeal for what rightly belongs to Him (everything
that He created even if it is entrusted to someone else, Ps.
24:1) and His holy nature (Ex. 34:14). God is love (goodness) or that which perfectly wills the good of its object
(1 John 4:16). God is truth or His very nature is truthful-
ness in that He is reliable, faithful, and stable (Deut. 32:4;
John 14:6). In contrast to these moral attributes, humans
are sinful in that their sin is unholy (1 Tim. 1:9, cf. 2 Tim.
3:2–5), sin is unrighteousness or injustices (Rom. 10:3),
sin is moral imperfection, sin is the presence of ungodly
jealousy, sin is being unloving (1 John 4:20), sin is being
untruthful (Ex. 20:16, Col. 3:9). In short, sin is being the
opposite of God (Table 3.2).

| God | Humans |
|---|---|
| God is Holy | Sin is Being Unholy |
| God is Righteousness | Sin is Unrighteousness |
| God is Perfect | Sin is Moral Imperfection |
| God is Jealous | Sin is Ungodly Jealousy |
| God is Love | Sin is Being Unloving |
| God is Truth | Sin is Being Untruthful |

Table 3.2

The process of sinning is explicitly identified in James 1:13–15: "Let no one say when he is tempted, 'I am being tempted by God'; for God cannot be tempted by evil, and He Himself does not tempt anyone. But each one is tempted when he is *carried away* and *enticed* by *his own lust*. Then when lust has *conceived*, it gives *birth to sin*; and when *sin is accomplished*, it brings forth *death*" (emphasis added).

James goes on to explain that we overcome sin by being doers of the word of God, not merely a hearer of the word (James 1:22–23). "But one who looks intently at the perfect law, the law of liberty, and abides by it, not having become a forgetful hearer but an effectual doer, this man will be blessed in what he does" (James 1:25). Paul also assures us,

> No temptation has overtaken you but such as is common to man; and God is faithful, who will not allow you to be tempted beyond what you are able, but with the temptation will provide the way of escape also, so that you will be able to endure it. (1 Cor. 10:13)

Paul also encourages us to speak truth to other believers and never cease being angry at sin.

> Therefore, laying aside falsehood, speak truth each one of you with his neighbor, for we are members of one another. Be angry, and yet do not sin; do not let the sun go down on your anger, and do not give the devil an opportunity. (Eph. 4:25–27)

Some have argued that God must have created sin, saying that

1) God created everything.
2) Sin is a real thing.
3) Therefore, God created sin.

It would seem we must either reject (1) or (2) in order to deny (3). It is true that God did create everything that is every substance; however, sin is not a substance. It is a privation or lack in a good substance. Sin exists only in something good, as a corruption of its goodness. Evil or sin is not a thing or substance; hence God did not create it. Instead, it is a privation, lack or corruption of essentially good things. We must also keep in mind the sovereignty of God and His providence. God is the one that is "upholding all things by the word of His power" (Heb. 1:3). God prevents some sins from happening (Gen. 20:6; 31:24; Ps. 19:13; 1 Cor. 11:30; 1 John 5:16) and God permits some sin to fulfill His own plan and good purposes (Ps. 81:12; Isa. 53:10).

Some have objected that God's absolute standard of perfection makes it irrational to demand mortal humans to comply. However, it must be kept in mind that Adam was created with the ability to adhere to the standard and was not tempted on moral matters, but on obedience to God. God cannot lower or diminish His ultimate standard (Heb. 6:18; 2 Tim. 2:13). The ultimate answer to the problem is God's enabling grace. It is impossible for us to please God in our sinful flesh (Isa. 64:6; Titus 3:5; Rom. 7:18; John 15:5). We cannot do it in our own strength, but with His grace it is possible (Phil. 2:13; 4:13; 1 Cor. 10:13). What we morally ought to do implies can, and we can only by God's grace.

### SUMMARY

God as the standard of all perfection Who cannot sin. However, He can permit sin which is not necessarily an evil. God created only good creatures with the goodness of free will. This was wrongly exercised against Him by the first human couple on earth. This first human sin was a free self–determined act exercised against the command of God. Sin is always an offence against God and falls short of God's perfect moral nature.

## Questions to Answer

1) What can God do and not do with respect to sin?
2) How did sin, according to the Bible, originate with angels and man?
3) What is the cause of Adam's sin?
4) What are the two basic kinds of sin according to the Bible?
5) How is sin to be dealt, according to the Bible, in the life of the believer?

# 4

## The Effects of Sin

*Therefore, just as through one man sin entered into the
world, and death through sin, and so death spread to all
men, because all sinned . . .*
*Romans 5:12*

As we have seen, God created the first human beings
in a state of perfection (Chapter 1). One of the per-
fections God gave was the power of free choice (Chapter
2). Adam and Eve exercised this freedom to disobey God
(Chapter 3). This wrong use of their free will resulted in a
state of human sinfulness that humans cannot reverse.

### THREE KINDS OF DEATH

The effects of Adam and Eve's sin resulted in three kinds of
death for the human race. The first is spiritual death. The
moment Adam sinned he experienced spiritual isolation,
that is separation from God Genesis 3:7–8 says, "Then
the eyes of both of them were opened, and they knew
that *they were naked*; . . . and the man and his wife *hid
themselves from the presence of the Lord God* among the

47

trees of the garden" (emphasis added). Every decedent of Adam, born of natural parents, is spiritually dead as well. John 3:3, 5–7 says,

> Jesus answered and said to him, "Truly, truly, I say to you, unless one is born again he cannot see the kingdom of God." . . . unless one is born of water and the Spirit he cannot enter into the kingdom of God. That which is born of the flesh is flesh, and that which is born of the Spirit is spirit. Do not be amazed that I said to you, 'You must be born again.'

Without this regeneration, every human being is spiritually dead in sin (cf. Titus 3:5–7).

The second is physical death. The moment Adam partook of the forbidden fruit he began to die physically Genesis 2:16–17 says,

> The Lord God commanded the man, saying, "From any tree of the garden you may eat freely; but from the tree of the knowledge of good and evil you shall not eat, for in the day that you eat from it you will surely die."

Physical death is the inevitable result of Adam's sin and for all his natural descendants except Christ.

Paul in Romans 5:12–14 writes,

> Therefore, just as through one man sin entered into the world, and death through sin, and so death spread to all men, because all sinned [in Adam] . . . death reigned from Adam until Moses, even over those who had not sinned in the likeness of the offense of Adam, who is a type of Him who was to come [Jesus]. (emphasis added)

Because all humans are already spiritually dead when physically born, they only actually undergo physical and eternal death in terms of experience. This implies that the spiritual death of everyone occurred in the *sin of Adam*.

The third is eternal death. This is the "second death" or eternal separation from God. If Adam had not accepted God's provision (Gen. 3:15–24) he would have eventually experienced "the second death," which is eternal separation from God. John wrote in Revelation 20:14–15,

> Then death and Hades were thrown into the lake of fire. This is the second death, the lake of fire. And if anyone's name was not found written in the book of life, he was thrown into the lake of fire.

As a result, those who are born only once (physically) will die twice (physically and eternally); however, those who are born twice (physically and spiritually) will die only once (physically). As Jesus says in John 11:26, "Everyone who lives and believes in Me will never die. Do you believe this?"

### Effects of Sin on Adam's Descendants

Adam's sin affected his offspring in that all have sinned "through one man" (Rom. 5:12). All of humanity was present and represented in Adam's sin. All were present potentially since every human is derived from the first human in terms of the same human nature passed on according to the Traducian view. All are present seminally (Heb. 7:9–10) since all biologically are fully derived from the first humans. And all are legally (judicially–legal) represented in Adam as the appointed head of the human race.

Adam had the God–given power of attorney for the whole human race. When he exercised it for ill, the consequences of his sin were directly imputed to all of his posterity. Romans 5:18–19 says,

> So then as through one transgression there resulted condemnation to all men, even so through one act of righteousness there resulted justification of life to all men. For as through the one man's disobedience the many were made sinners, even so through the obedience of the One the many will be made righteous.

All stand guilty before God for what Adam did on our behalf. The "many" (= all) were not made sinners *actually*, but were *potentially* and *legally* present in Adam so as to receive the imputation of the consequences of his sin. The judicial consequences of Adam's sin were imputed to all his natural offspring. Paul tells us that Christ, "The last Adam" (1 Cor. 15:45) revoked what Adam did, making every human legally and potentially savable.

The transmissional effects of Adam's sin include imputation and inheritance. Imputed sin is that fallenness and depravity were imputed or attributed to his descendants *directly* and *immediately*. Inherited sin is the original sin nature that is transmitted *indirectly* and *mediately* to everyone generated naturally from Adam. This is the doctrine of original sin. Paul in Ephesians (2:1–3) says, "And you were dead in your trespasses and sins, in which you formerly walked according to the course of this world, according to the prince of the power of the air, of the spirit that is now working in the sons of disobedience." Hence, we are sinners by nature because we are born in it and because we inevitably do what comes naturally, viz., we sin.

How is this sin nature transmitted? *How* it is transmitted is open to theological debate. But that it is transmitted is undebatable, since this is what the Bible teaches. This best explanation of how it is transmitted is according to the Traducian view (Chapter 1). The view can be summarized as follows:

1.  God directly created Adam's perfect (sinless) soul.

2.  Each soul, since Adam, comes into this world by natural generations from his or her parents.

3.  God cannot directly create fallen (sinful) souls.

4.  Therefore, inherited sin arises indirectly from God by way of a fallen human being.

The judicial or legal effects of Adam's sin indicate that Adam has the God given power of attorney for the whole human race. As Paul says in Romans 5:18–19: "So then as through one transgression there resulted condemnation to all men, even so through one act of righteousness there resulted justification of life to all men. For as through the one man's disobedience the many were made sinners, even so through the obedience of the One the many will be made righteous." All were not made sinners actually at the moment Adam sinned, since they did not actually exist at the time. However, they were potentially and legally present in Adam, and, as such, received the imputation of the consequences of his sin.

The effects of sin on our relationship with God was immediate spiritual separation from God. Death is separation and spiritual death is spiritual separation from God. This spiritual death should not be misunderstood as human beings so depraved they cannot understand or respond to God's message. Paul makes it quite clear that salvation from spiritual death comes "through faith" (Eph. 2:8–9). Other figures of speech describe the *total depravity* of the sinner as *polluted* in need of purification/ cleansing (Titus 2:14; Heb. 10:22), *sick* in need of healing (Isa. 53:5; Mark 2:17), in the *dark* in need of light

(John 8:12; 12:36). The sinner is not *dead* in the sense of not being able to by God's grace, understand and accept salvation. Sick people can receive a cure, a dirty person can embrace cleansing and a person in the dark can embrace the light. Indeed, the sinner is incapable of doing these things by himself (in his own strength). Because he lacks spiritual life, he needs the aid of God's grace. *Total depravity means the total inability to achieve/obtain the solution to our sin by ourselves, not the total inability to accept it from God.*

Adam's act of disobedience, since it was a sin or trespass that resulted in "condemnation" (Rom. 5:12, 17, 18) resulted in guilt and shame. Guilt coming from the reality of his failure and shame coming from the recognition of the failure (Gen. 3:7).

Adam not only lost his relationship with God, he also lost his fellowship with God. Adam no longer wanted to talk with his Creator but instead hid from Him (Gen. 3:8; cf. 1 John 1:6–7). His relationship with other people was also disturbed. This horizontal as well as vertical effect of sin is evident in that Adam blamed Eve for his situation (Gen. 3:12) and is evident in the disrupted sibling relationship in which Cain out of anger killed his brother Able (Gen. 4:1–8). Sin also affected Adam's relationship with the environment. Prior to the Fall, Adam and Eve were to "subdue" the earth (Gen. 1:28) not destroy it or pollute it. After the Fall, he was put under bondage to his environment. Thorns and thistles appeared. He had to work by the sweat of his brow. Death became a fact of life (Gen. 3:17–19; cf. Rom. 8:20–21).

Indeed, the effects of sin on fallen human beings are so great that without God's common grace society would be unlivable and salvation unattainable. Without God's common grace: the judicial effects of sin would produce overwhelming guilt (Rom. 5:12–21). The blinding effects of sin would make it impossible to recognize evil as such (2 Cor. 4:4). The deceiving effects of sin would make rational thought and action virtually impossible (Jer. 17:9). The debasing effects of sin would be destructive of self and others (Rom 1:21–32). The corrupting effects of sin would produce moral decay and that dominates society (Eph. 2:1–3) The debilitative effects of sin would make performance of social good unachievable (Rom. 3:10–18). Only God's common grace to unsaved persons makes living in this corrupt world possible. This common grace is provided through natural revelation (Rom. 1:19–20), the moral law (Rom. 2:12–20), God's image in humans (Gen. 9:6), marriage (Heb. 13:4), the family structure (Eph. 6:1–4), human government (Rom. 13:1–7) and many other non–redemptive means.

### Effects of Sin on Humans

The biblical account of the effects of sin upon human beings shows that it is vast and pervasive. It touches the very core of our being, corrupting the totality of human nature—nothing is left untouched.

There are effects of sin on the image of God in humans. This image of God in humans is effaced but not erased. Sin effaces this image, but does not erase the image of God; it is marred but not eliminated. The fallen state includes the image of God. Gen. 9:6 says, "Whoever sheds man's blood, By man his blood shall be shed, For in the image of God He made man." If unsaved people were not still in the image of God, this prohibition against murder would make no sense. Indeed, we are instructed not to curse other human beings, since they are in God's image according to James 3:9–10: "With it [tongue] we bless our Lord and Father, and with it we curse men, who have been made in the likeness of God . . ." The image of God is marred but not eliminated.

Sin is extensive, but it is not intensive. Sin is pervasive, extending to every dimension of our being (body, soul, will). It is in this sense that we are "totally depraved." But it does not mean humans are as sinful as they could be, apart from Christ we are not as good as we should be. Sin does penetrate and permeates our whole being. Humans are born wholly, not partially, depraved; that is, every aspect of our being is affected by sin. No element of human nature is unaffected by inherited evil, even though no aspect is completely destroyed by it. Total depravity taken too far eliminates the ability for one to be depraved. Hence, *total depravity* cannot mean "one's ability to know and choose good over evil is destroyed." If it does, then the person has no access to the good (only evil is available to him). Their volition has been eliminated and is no longer able to sin. Taken too far one's ability to ever know and choose good over evil is destroyed. What has no moral capacity and ability has no moral responsibility.

The noetic (relating to the mind) effects of sin on humans entail that depravity brings spiritual darkness and blindness (Rom. 1:28). Second Corinthians 4:4 says, "In whose case the god of this world has blinded the minds of the unbelieving so that they might not see the light of the gospel of the glory of Christ, who is the image of God." John 12:46 says, "I [Jesus] have come as Light into the world, so that everyone who believes in Me will not remain in darkness" (cf. Eph. 5:8; Acts 26:18). The purpose of salvation is to open the eyes of unbelievers, turn them from darkness to light; from the power of Satan to God (Acts 26:18).

The volitional (relating to the will) entails that humans cannot, unmoved by divine grace, seek God. Romans 3:11 says, "There is none who understands. There is none who seeks for God." Hence, we cannot initiate salvation (John 1:13) and we cannot attain salvation. Paul says in Romans 9:16: "So then it does not depend on the man who wills or the man who runs, but on God who has mercy."

We are free in things below in social and moral choices. This freedom is evident in our choice of a mate (1 Cor. 7:39). This freedom is described as having "no constraint," "authority over his own will" and "decided this in his own heart (v. 37). It is spontaneous and not forced (Philem. 14).

We are also free to receive or reject the gift of salvation. This is implied everywhere in the gospel call (John 3:16; Acts 16:31; 17:30). John 1:12 says, "But as many as received Him, to them He gave the right to become children of God, even to those who believe in His name." We are offered salvation as a gift. Unsaved people have a free choice regarding the reception or rejection of God's gift of salvation (Rom. 6:23). Jesus lamented the condition of those who rejected Him: "Jerusalem, Jerusalem, . . .How often I wanted to gather your children together, the way a hen gathers her chicks under her wings, and you were unwilling." Indeed, God desires that all unsaved people to change their mind (i.e., repent), for He "is patient toward you, not wishing for any to perish but for *all to come to repentance*" (2 Peter 3:9, emphasis added). Over and over, throughout Scripture "belief" is declared to be something we are accountable to embrace (Deut. 30:19; Josh. 24:15; John 6:69; 8:24; 9:36, 38; 10:25). Jesus said, "He who believes in [Me] is not judged; *he who does not believe has been judged already, because he has not believed* in the name of the only begotten Son of God" (John 3:18, emphasis added).

The act of faith is prompted and aided by God but He does not perform it or choose for us. First Corinthians 2:4–6 says, "And my message and my preaching were not in persuasive words of wisdom, but in demonstration of the Spirit and of power so that your faith would not rest on the wisdom of men, but on the power of God. Yet we do speak wisdom among those who are mature; a wisdom, however, not of this age nor of the rulers of this age, who are passing away" (cf. 2 Cor. 3:5).

So, what does it mean to have a fallen human nature? It means we are born this way (Ps. 51:5; 58:3). It means we are born with the propensity to sin and the necessity to die. It is our nature for us to sin, an inclination; it does not have to be taught. Sin is inevitable, given an opportunity to manifest itself and we are incapable of saving ourselves; because we sin by nature and practice; thus, making it impossible to enter God's perfect heaven.

What does it *not* mean to have a fallen human nature? It does not mean that everyone is as sinful as they could be. It does not mean sin is excusable since we are responsible. It does not mean that we are unable to avoid sin since we are accountable (Rom. 14:12; Rev. 20:12). It does not mean that any particular sin is inescapable for believers (1 Cor. 10:13) and unbelievers (Titus 2:11–13). And it does not mean that we have no choice in our salvation.

God not only wants all to be saved (1 Tim. 2:4; 2 Peter 3:9), He provides the ability for all who desire it (Phil. 2:13). Our free choice does not *initiate* (1 John 3:19) and cannot *attain* (John 1:13) the unmerited gift of salvation, but by God's grace (Eph. 2:8–9) our will can receive it (John 1:12; 3:16–18).

So, what *does* it mean to have a fallen nature? First, it means we are born this way (Ps. 51:5; cf. 58:3). Second, it means that it is natural for us to sin. It is not merely an acquired habit; it is a basic inclination. It does not have to be taught. Third, it means one will inevitably sin; given the opportunity, sin will manifest itself. Fourth, it means we are incapable of saving ourselves. No matter how good we try to be, we are still sinners by nature and practice and therefore cannot enter God's perfect heaven without Jesus Christ. In brief, we are not simply sinners because we sin; we sin because we are sinners.

What does it *not* mean to have a fallen nature? First, it does not mean we are as sinful as we could be. Instead, it means that we are not as good as we should be. Second, our fallen nature does not mean that sin is excusable. We are responsible for every sin we commit. Third, it does not mean we are unable to avoid sin. Otherwise we would not be responsible for our sins—but we are (Rom. 14:12). Fourth, it does not mean that any particular sin is inescapable. Sin in general is inevitable, but no sin in particular is unavoidable. God's grace is always available to resist sin. This includes the believer (1 Cor. 10:13) and the unbeliever (Titus 2:11–13). Finally, having a fallen nature does not mean we have no choice in our salvation. The unaided human will cannot believe unto salvation, nonetheless, all who are willing to receive God's gift of salvation are aided by His grace to this end. God not only want all to be saved, He provides the ability for all who desire it (Phil. 2:13). Our free choice does not initiate (1 John 3:19) and cannot attain (John 1:13) the unmerited gift of salvation, but by God's grace (Eph. 2:8–9) our will can receive it (John 1:12; 3:16–18).

## THE EXTENT OF SIN (DEPRAVITY)

There are four views of depravity. The first view is that of Pelagius, a British monk (c. 354–c. 420 A.D.). His view was condemned at the Council of Carthage (416–418 A.D.) because he held that human beings are born innocent, just as Adam was created innocent. This view says humans inherit no sin from Adam, so they are able to obey God. The only thing Adam bequeathed to humanity is a bad example. Only our own sins are imputed to us as opposed to ours and Adams. Even physical death is not the result of Adam's sin, we are just created mortal. The image of God in this view is untarnished, and grace is not needed for salvation.

Jacob (James) Arminius (1560–1609) said that imputed sin entails that all are born with a weakened nature since they are potentially or seminally in Adam and bent toward sin. He taught that all are deprived but can by God's grace obey God. Some who follow this view do add grace. The image of God is effaced. Death entails all are spiritually separated from God from birth, which does not entail the loss of the human ability to respond. God's grace does not work irresistibly on all, but only on the elect. It works sufficiently on all awaiting their free cooperation before it becomes saving.

John Calvin (1509–1564) from which Calvinism comes has two forms: strong and moderate. The two views are contrasted in Table 4.1.

| Position | Strong (Extreme) Calvinism | Moderate Calvinism |
|---|---|---|
| Grace | Operative | Cooperative |
| Actions | Monergistic | Synergistic |
| Recipient | Passive object | Active agent |
| Free act | No | Yes |
| Resistibility | Irresistible on the unwilling | Irresistible on the willing. |

Table 4.1

The strong view, following Theodore Beza (1519–1605) and the Synod of Dort (1618–1619), was adopted by Reformed theology. It asserts that imputed sin entails that all human beings sinned in Adam (legally or naturally) and inherit a sinful nature. Depravity is total in the sense of extent and intensity. The image of God in humans is for all intents and purposes destroyed. Fallen humans are "dead" in sin (Eph. 2:1). Death entails that all cannot understand or respond to the gospel since they are dead (from birth) in the sense of being unable to respond. And the grace of God must be irresistible grace and regenerate the sinner (even against his will) to be saved. Only the elect have irresistible grace that involves no choice to understand and believe. It is often understood under the acrostic TULIP: T–otal Depravity; U–nconditional Election; L–imited Atonement; I–rresistable Grace, and P–erseverence of the Saints (that all the regenerate will persevere to the end and be saved).

The moderate view, sees imputed sin as all human beings sinned in Adam legally or naturally and therefore inherit a sinful nature. Depravity entails that all are depraved totally in extent, but not in intensity. Hence, we can understand and obey by God's saving grace. The image of God is effaced but not erased. Death entails that all are spiritually separated from God (from birth) but does not involve the loss of human reason and free will, although these can be influenced by sin. Guilt can only be overcome by God's saving grace. Grace is not merely sufficient for all; it is efficient for the elect. Irresistible grace is only on the willing, not the unwilling.

In summary, Pelagianism is contrary to orthodoxy since it sees humans as innocent at birth and able to respond to God. Arminianism (or Semi–Pelagianism) sees humans as depraved but able to cooperate with God. Calvinism has two forms: 1) Strong Calvinism sees humans as totally depraved, to the extent that the image of God in humans is destroyed and humans cannot cooperate with God. 2) Moderate Calvinism sees humans as totally depraved with the image of God in humans effaced, and humans can cooperate with God. The views are contrasted in the following table (4.2).

| | Pelagianism | Arminianism | Moderate Calvinism | Strong Calvinism |
|---|---|---|---|---|
| **State at birth** | Innocent | Depraved | Total Depraved (extensively) | Totally Depraved (intensively) |
| **Ability** | Can obey God | Can cooperate with God | Can cooperate with God | Can't cooperate with God |
| **Guilt** | None | Potential | Judicial (and/or actual) | Actual (and/or judicial) |
| **"In Adam" (Rom. 5:12)** | Not at all (rather, we sinned like Adam) | Potentially (or seminally) | Legally (and/or naturally) | Naturally (and/or legally) |
| **What is inherited from Adam** | Bad example | Propensity to sin; necessity to die. | Propensity to sin; necessity to die. | Necessity to sin; necessity to die |
| **Deaths incurred** | Spiritual and eternal | Physical and spiritual | Physical, spiritual, and eternal | Physical, spiritual, and eternal |
| **What is imputed** | One's own sin | One's own sin (we ratify Adam's sin) | One's own sin and Adam's sin | One's own sin and Adam's sin. |
| **Spiritual image of God** | Retained | Effaced | Effaced | Erased (logical outworking of view) |
| **Effect of grace** | None | Sufficient for all | Irresistible on the willing | Irresistible on the unwilling |

Table 4.2

Can everyone believe? Salvation is a gift for all men, and all are responsible to believe. By God's grace, they are able to believe. John 3:16–18 says, "For God so loved the world that He gave His only begotten Son, that whoever believes in Him shall not perish, but have eternal life. For God did not send the Son into the world to judge the world, but that the world might be saved through Him. He who believes in Him is not judged; he who does not believe has been judged already, because he has not believed in the name of the only begotten Son of God." But as stated in John 12:37–40, some will not believe:

> But though He had performed so many signs before them, yet they were not believing in Him. This was to fulfill the word of Isaiah the prophet which he spoke: "Lord, who has believed our report? And to whom has the arm of the Lord been revealed?" For this reason they could not believe, for Isaiah said again, "He has blinded their eyes and He hardened their heart, so that they would not see with their eyes and perceive with their heart, and be converted and I would heal them.

The context of this passage is hardhearted Jews who witnessed Jesus' miracles and were called upon repeatedly to believe (John 8:24–36). The responsibility is still to believe since God held them responsible for not believing. Their own stubborn unbelief caused their blindness (John 8:24). We also know that the work of Satan shows men can believe (2 Cor. 4:3–4). As it makes no sense for Satan to blind the minds of the unbeliever if they cannot believe. Faith is not a gift offered only to the elect. As Ephesians 2:8–9 "For by grace you have been saved through faith; and that not of yourselves, it is the gift of God."

Can anyone believe without God's special grace? The answer is no! Faith is possible for the unsaved, but no one can have saving faith without the aid of God's grace. John. 6:44 says, "No one can come to Me unless the Father who sent Me draws him; and I will raise him up on the last day." Gracious action of salvation is not monergistic–or an act of God alone–it is synergistic or an act of God and our free choice. Grace is exercised on an active agent, not a passive object.

## Summary

God cannot cause sin, but He can permit sin. By Adam's self–determined act of disobedience he plunged the entire human race into sin, such that through Adam sin is imputed and inherited. As a result, humans are born separated spiritually from God and will suffer physical death, and unless born again will suffer eternal death. Such depravity effaced the image of God in man, but did not erase it. Sin is extensive, but not intensive. Everyone can believe and cooperate with God's grace, but not everyone will.

### Questions to Answer

1. What are the three kinds of death that resulted from sin?
2. What are the effects of sin on Adam's descendants?
3. What does it mean and not mean to have a fallen human nature?
4. What are the different views of depravity?
5. What Bible verses show that God's grace and human belief are needed for salvation?

# 5

## The Defeat of Sin

*He made Him who knew no sin to be sin on our behalf,*
*so that we might become the righteousness of God in*
*Him.*
*2 Corinthians 5:21*

God's divine plan, from eternity, is to defeat sin instead of annihilating it. He chose to execute the plan to defeat it progressively instead of instantaneously. At the result of God's plan is to defeat evil without destroying our God given freedom and at the same time perfecting free creatures.

### The Divine Plan to Defeat Evil

God's plan to defeat evil was devised from eternity. God created free creatures (angels and human beings). In so doing, God permitted evil because in so doing He would conquer it and allow for a greater good. God, since He is an eternal Being, willed His plan from eternity in accordance with His divine attributes. Since God is all knowing, He knew how everything would turnout from the beginning.

Since God is all–loving, it is assured He would honor the free will He gave to creatures. Since God is all –powerful, it is certain that He would accomplish all He sets out to do. God's freedom guarantees He was not influenced or forced to do what He did. Since He is all wise, He would choose the wisest means to accomplish His ends.

Some ask, if God knew evil would occur, why did He create at all? To answer this, we must show that this world, where evil is possible and actually happened is superior to all other alternative worlds. The alternatives are 1) God could not have created; 2) God could have created non–free creatures. 3) God could have created a free world where no one chooses to sin; 4) God could have created a free world where no one is allowed to sin; 5) God could have created a world where sin occurs but all are saved.

Alternatives, 1 and 2 cannot be morally better than this moral world. No world is not morally better than some world and a non–free world is not morally better than a free world. Alternative 3 may be logically possible, but not actually achievable. And even if possible may not be the best world possible, that is achieving the greatest good. Alternative 4 appears contradictory, since one cannot be free to sin but is not allowed to sin. Alternative 5 likewise is conceivable, but may not be achievable if everyone is truly free and may be ultimately morally inferior.

Hence, it is indeed possible that this present evil world is the best possible means of obtaining the best world achievable given 1) some are saved and some are lost and 2) sin is defeated and a greater good is achieved. That is, God chose to permit a world that is not the best possible world in order to achieve one that is. While our world is not the best world possible, it is the best way possible to achieve the best of all possible worlds, where everyone is freely choosing his own destiny and sin is forever defeated and righteousness reigns eternally. The very nature of God assures us that evil will eventually be defeated:

1) God is all–loving and wants to defeat evil
2) God is all–powerful and can defeat evil.
3) Evil is not yet defeated.
4) Hence, evil will yet be defeated (in the future).

The fact that God is all–good and all–powerful guarantees this conclusion. Since God is all–wise we can be sure He chooses the best means to defeating all evil. This present world is not the best of all possible worlds, nonetheless, it must be the best means to the best world. A world in which evil is permitted is the best kind of world to permit as a means to producing the best kind of world—one that has no evil in it. According to the Bible, this world is our promised destiny (Rev. 21).

## The Execution of God's Plan

Instead of annihilating all evil immediately, which would require the destruction of all good made possible by freedom as well, the all–wise God decided to defeat evil gradually, through–out the ages. Writing of Christ's coming kingdom, Paul affirmed "with a view to an administration [or dispensation] suitable to the fullness of the times, that is, the summing up of all things in Christ, things in the heavens and things on the earth" (Eph. 1:10). In each age or period from Adam to Christ's return, God orchestrates different conditions to test to see if humans will obey Him (Table 5.1).

| Dispensations | Scripture | Responsibilities/Test | Result/Judgment(s) |
|---|---|---|---|
| Innocence | Gen. 1–3 | Given a state of innocent purity, not know good or evil, humans did not obey God's command. | Sin, curses, spiritual and physical death |
| Moral Conscience | Gen. 6–9 | Fallen humans, given a conscience to inform them what was right and wrong, disobeyed. | God sent the Flood |
| Human Government | Gen. 9–11 | God established human government to enforce obedience. | Destroyed their tower and dispersed them by confounding their languages |
| Promise | Gen. 12 | God chose one nation through Abraham and gave them the Promised Land to dwell. | Egyptian bondage |
| Law | Ex. 19 | God gave them the Law through Moses, but they disobeyed through idolatry and immorality. | Assyrian and Babylonian Captivities |
| Grace | Acts 2 | God's unlimited benevolence was poured out to the masses through the Cross. | Great Tribulation |
| Millennium | Rev. 19–20 | God's promised reign of the Messiah is visible through a literal kingdom, human freedom is tested with Satan bound for "thousand years." | Great White Throne Judgment |

Table 5.1

The point is not how many of these periods existed or even what they should be called, instead it is the distinct conditions God has (or will) give to test humankind in working out His plan to defeat evil. Through periods of history humanity is divinely examined, God will have defeated sin by permitting it in virtually every possible way. Proving under each case, that human freedom, even with God's guidance and intervention always freely rebels against God. Thus, demonstrating God's ultimate glory in that 1) sin is always wrong, 2) God is always right and 3) evil is justly put away forever.

God's plan to defeat evil was (and is being) gradually executed in seven primary stages:

1) the creation of free creatures;
2) the fall of humankind;
3) the preparation of the Savior;
4) the incarnation of the Savior;
5) the present session of the Savior (in heaven);
6) the return and reign of the Savior (the final judgment);
7) the new heaven and new earth.

**1) The creation of free creatures.** God knows the end from the beginning (Isa. 46:10). Before God even created he knew the fall of humanity and planned for our salvation. Knowing this, he created humans innocent, perfect and with free will (Gen. 2:16), holding them responsible for their choices (Gen. 2:16–17).

**2) The fall of humankind.** Nothing catches an all-knowing Mind by surprise. From eternity God knew the fall, permitting Adam and Eve to sin was part of God's plan to defeat evil. Paul said, "just as He chose us in Him before the foundation of the world, that we would be holy and blameless before Him" (Eph. 1:4).

3) **The preparation of the Savior.** Immediately after the Fall, God announced His eternal plan to provide salvation for all humankind. To the serpent (Devil) who tempted Adam and Eve, He said, "And I will put enmity between you and the woman, and between your seed and her seed; He shall bruise you on the head, and you shall bruise him on the heel" (Gen. 3:5). The Savior is the Seed of the woman, He ultimately–fatally–crushed the Serpent's head. Christ did this *officially* on the Cross (Col. 2:14) and will do *actually* when He returns (Rom. 16:20; Rev. 20:10). The rest of the Old Testament is the preparation for the coming Savior. In the books of the law (Genesis through Deuteronomy) God laid the *foundation* for Christ by calling into existence the holy nation through which the Promised Seed would come. In the historical books (Joshua through Nehemiah) He made *provision* by obtaining the Holy Land. In the poetical books (Job through Ecclesiastes) *aspiration* for Christ was made. The prophetic books (Isaiah through Malachi) earnestly proclaimed the *expectation* for Christ.

4) **The incarnation of the Savior.** The anticipation of the Old Testament became the realization of the New Testament. Paul says, "But when the fullness of the time came, God sent forth His Son, born of a woman, born under the Law, so that He might redeem those who were under the Law, that we might receive the adoption as sons" (Gal. 4:4–5). The eternal Word assumed temporal flesh. He became incarnate to 1) fulfill prophecy, 2) manifest deity and 3) redeem humanity. The Gospel of John says,

> In the beginning was the Word, and the Word was with God, and the Word was God. . . . And the Word became flesh, and dwelt among us, and we saw His glory, glory as of the only begotten

from the Father, full of grace and truth. (John 1:1; 14)

The Gospels detail the historic *manifestation* of Jesus Christ. Acts *chronicles* the spread of the Gospel of Christ; the Epistles establish the *interpretation* and *application* of Christ; and Revelation reveals the final *consummation* in Christ.

Christ's as Priest (Mark 10:45) made a sacrificial death that was substitutionary. Jesus Christ said, "I came that they may have life, and have it abundantly. . . and I lay down My life for the sheep (John 10:10, 15; cf. Isa. 53:4–7; 2 Cor. 5:21).

Christ's physical resurrection is the pinnacle of God's plan of redemption. Paul wrote, "He who was delivered over because of our transgressions, and was raised because of our justification" (Rom. 4:25). The resurrection of Christ is the culmination point of all four Gospels: Matthew, Mark, Luke and John. It is the dominate theme of apostolic preaching (Acts 2, 13). As Paul said, it is the heart of the gospel (1 Cor. 15:1–8) and one cannot be saved without believing in it (1 Cor. 15:14–19).

Christ's bodily ascension into heaven is the completion and final acceptance of His finished work of salvation. This was announced in advance, "I am returning to my Father" (John 20:17). Jesus explained the reason, as Luke wrote:

> And behold, I am sending forth the promise of My Father upon you; but you are to stay in the city until you are clothed with power from on high." . . . And He led them out as far as Bethany, and He lifted up His hands and blessed them. While He was blessing them, He parted from them and was carried up into heaven. (Luke 24:49–51)

Jesus came from and returned to his Father (Eph. 4:9–10). Just as Jesus in His humiliation descended to the grave, so in His exultation He ascended into heaven. Paul wrote in Philippians (2:8–11):

> Being found in appearance as a man, He humbled Himself by becoming obedient to the point of death, even death on a cross. For this reason also, *God highly exalted Him, and bestowed on Him the name which is above every name,* so that at the name of Jesus every knee will bow, of those who are in heaven and on earth and under the earth, and that every tongue will confess that Jesus Christ is Lord, to the glory of God the Father. (Emphasis added)

This was necessary to have the Holy Spirit descend to indwell and empower the disciples (John 16:10, 28). His ascension was the literal, visible rising of His resurrected body. It was not invisible or a transformation into an invisible body. It was simply the passing out of sight of His physical resurrected body. Acts 1:9–11 says,

> And after He had said these things, He was lifted up while they were looking on, and a cloud received Him out of their sight. And as they were gazing intently into the sky while He was going, behold, two men in white clothing stood beside them. They also said, "Men of Galilee, why do you stand looking into the sky? This Jesus, who has been taken up from you into heaven, will come in just the same way as you have watched Him go into heaven."

**5) The present session of the Savior (in heaven).** Christ's present priestly session on behalf of believers is described by John:

> My little children, I am writing these things to you so that you may not sin. And if anyone sins, we have an Advocate with the Father, Jesus Christ the righteous; and He Himself is the propitiation

for our sins; and not for ours only, but also for those of the whole world. (1 John 2:1–2)

Satan is the accuser of God's people. Revelation 12:10 (cf. Job 1–2) says,

Now the salvation, and the power, and the kingdom of our God and the authority of His Christ have come, *for the accuser of our brethren has been thrown down, he who accuses them before our God day and night.* (Emphasis added)

Christ is our Advocate who counters by pleading with His Father the efficacy of His blood, that was shed for our sins (Heb. 7:17, 22–26).

For it is attested of Him, "You are a priest forever According to the order of Melchizedek." . . . so much the more also Jesus has become the guarantee of a better covenant. The former priests, on the one hand, existed in greater numbers because they were prevented by death from continuing, but Jesus, on the other hand, because He continues forever, holds His priesthood permanently. Therefore He is able also to save forever those who draw near to God through Him, since He always lives to make intercession for them. For it was fitting for us to have such a high priest, holy, innocent, undefiled, separated from sinners and exalted above the heavens.

It is Christ who because He is truly human can sympathize with our human frailties (Heb. 4:14–15) who was tempted in all points as we are and because of His present session can provide a "way out" for us (1 Cor. 10:13).

6) **The return and reign of the Savior (the final judgment).** Jesus is not only fulfilling the role of a Prophet and Priest for His people, He one day literally (actually, physically) will be King over them. Jesus said,

> Truly I say to you, that you who have followed Me, in the regeneration when the Son of Man will sit on His glorious throne, you also shall sit upon twelve thrones, judging the twelve tribes of Israel. (Matt. 19:28)

This reign will be for a thousand years, according to Revelation (20:4),

> Then I saw thrones, and they sat on them, and judgment was given to them. And I saw the souls of those who had been beheaded because of their testimony of Jesus and because of the word of God, and those who had not worshiped the beast or his image, and had not received the mark on their forehead and on their hand; and they came to life and reigned with Christ for a thousand years.

This is followed by the final judgment before the Great White Throne:

> Then I saw a great white throne and Him who sat upon it, from whose presence earth and heaven fled away, and no place was found for them. And I saw the dead, the great and the small, standing before the throne, and books were opened; and another book was opened, which is the book of life; and the dead were judged from the things which were written in the books, according to their deeds. And the sea gave up the dead which were in it, and death and Hades gave up the dead which were in them; and they were judged, every one of them according to their deeds. Then death and Hades were thrown into the lake of fire. This is the second death, the lake of fire. And if anyone's name was not found written in the book of life, he was thrown into the lake of fire. (Rev. 20:11–15).

7) **The new heaven and new earth.** This is the final state in which all evil is permanently removed, perfection prevails. Revelation (21:1–4) describes it.

> Then I saw a new heaven and a new earth; for
> the first heaven and the first earth passed away,
> and there is no longer any sea. And I saw the holy
> city, new Jerusalem, coming down out of heaven
> from God, made ready as a bride adorned for
> her husband. And I heard a loud voice from the
> throne, saying, "Behold, the tabernacle of God is
> among men, and He will dwell among them, and
> they shall be His people, and God Himself will be
> among them, and He will wipe away every tear
> from their eyes; and there will no longer be any
> death; there will no longer be any mourning, or
> crying, or pain; the first things have passed away.

Peter describes this great event in terms of how we should now live.

> But the day of the Lord will come like a thief, in
> which the heavens will pass away with a roar and
> the elements will be destroyed with intense heat,
> and the earth and its works will be burned up.
> Since all these things are to be destroyed in this
> way, what sort of people ought you to be in holy
> conduct and godliness, looking for and hastening
> the coming of the day of God, because of which
> the heavens will be destroyed by burning, and
> the elements will melt with intense heat! But
> according to His promise we are looking for new
> heavens and a new earth, in which righteousness
> dwells. (2 Peter 3:10–13; cf. Isa. 65:17–25)

## THE RESULT OF GOD'S PLAN

There is a distinction to make between the *official* defeat of sin, which was at the Cross (Col. 2:14; Heb. 2:14) and the *actual* defeat of sin, which will be at Christ's return. The result of God's plan involves the defeat of sin for the believer and the defeat of Satan.

### The Defeat of Sin for the Believer

For the believer, there are three stages in the overall battle to defeat sin. *Justification* is deliverance from the penalty of sin which is a past action for all believers, accomplished at the Cross and applied to them once they believe. *Sanctification* is the deliverance from the power of sin. It is a present and continuous process of believers becoming Christ like which is accomplished by the Holy Spirit's power and presence. *Glorification* is the deliverance from the presence of sin that takes place at Christ's return. It is important to see this as the defeat, not the destruction, of sin. Sin, in the sinner, will continue forever in hell. God defeats sin without destroying the sinner. So, it is important to answer what it does and does not mean to defeat sin.

What does the defeat of sin *not* mean? It does not mean that God will annihilate sinners. This would be an attack on God's own immortal image which all sinners bear, even in hell. For God to snuff out of existence people who do not love Him in return is contrary to the nature of an all–loving God. Rather, God will allow even those who hate Him to have their own way.

What *does* the defeat of sin mean? It means everlasting torment. Sin against the eternal God demands an eternal consequence. Because God's justice is forever just He cannot overlook sin forever. Now, good and evil exist side by side. But there must be an eternal separation of righteousness from sin which entails an eternal separation of the saved from the lost. Matthew's Gospel says,

> The Son of Man will send forth His angels, and they will gather out of His kingdom all stumbling blocks, and those who commit lawlessness, and will throw them into the furnace of fire; in that place there will be weeping and gnashing of teeth. (Matt. 13:41–42)

What frustrates good people is evil, and what frustrates evil people is good. The final solution demands a preeminent separation, where there will be no more evil to frustrate good persons and no more good to frustrate evil persons. Each will have it according to their respective wills: Sin will be defeated in the saved since they will be rescued from its very presence, and sin will also be defeated in the unsaved, since they will no longer be able to spread it to others. The infection of evil will be forever halted by its everlasting quarantine. Therefore, the good will be forever preserved from evil's deadly effects.

Evil is defeated because the good is actually victorious over it. Good can no longer be contaminated by it, and the righteous will reign while the wicked are in pain. The good will be unshackled from the presence of sin, and the evil will be forever enslaved by it.

> [God] will wipe away every tear from their eyes; and there will no longer be any death; there will no longer be any mourning, or crying, or pain; the first things have passed away. (Rev. 21:4)

**The Defeat of Satan and His Demons**

Satan, like the antichrist he inspires, "opposes and exalts himself above every so–called god or object of worship, so that he takes his seat in the temple of God, displaying himself as being God" (2 Thess. 2:4). He opposes God's plan and His people (Rev. 12:10). Satan causes doubt, denial, disobedience, deception, and the destruction of God's people and plan (2 Cor. 11:14). John wrote, "The Son of God appeared for this purpose, to destroy the works of the devil" (1 John 3:8).

The defeat of Satan, similar to the defeat of sin, is not accomplished with one blow. It is gradual. It was promised from the beginning when God said to the serpent, "And I will put enmity between you and the woman, and between your seed and her seed; *He shall crush you on the head*, and you shall bruise him on the heel" (Gen. 3:15, emphasis added). This was officially accomplished when Christ died on the cross and rose again. Paul says,

> [He] having forgiven us all our transgressions, having canceled out the certificate of debt consisting of decrees against us, which was hostile to us; and He has taken it out of the way, having nailed it to the cross. When *He had disarmed the rulers and authorities*, He made a public display of them, having *triumphed over them through the cross*. (Col. 2:14–15, emphasis added)

While the serpent was biting the heel of the Savior (by His crucifixion), the Savior was crushing the head of the serpent (by His resurrection). Satan bit the humanity of Christ, but got caught on His deity. As Hebrews says, "since the children share in flesh and blood, He Himself likewise also partook of the same, *that through death He might render powerless him who had the power of death, that is, the devil*" (Heb. 2:14, emphasis added). In a similar correspondence the three stages of salvation in a believer's life, the defeat of Satan also involves three stages: *Officially*, it occurred on the Cross; *Practically*, it is occurring through the purification of believers; and *Actually*, it will occur upon Christ's return. Satan was defeated officially or legally by the death of Christ (Rom. 3–5). He is being defeated practically in our lives when we resist him by the power of the Cross (Rom. 6–7). And He will be defeated finally and ultimately when Christ returns (Rom. 8), redeeming our bodies from death (Rom. 8:22–23). As Paul promised, "The God of peace will soon crush Satan under your feet. The grace of our Lord Jesus be with you" (Rom. 16:20).

The final defeat of Satan and his demons has two main aspects. First, is the judgment that separates of the sheep (believers) from the goats (unbelievers) prior to the millennial kingdom and reign of Christ on the earth (Matt. 25:32–34; 41). Second, during the millennial kingdom, the Devil is bound for the 1000 years according to Revelation (20:1–3). Upon his release, Satan is finally judged and permanently defeated:

> When the thousand years are completed, Satan will be released from his prison, and will come out to deceive the nations which are in the four corners of the earth . . . And the *devil who deceived them was thrown into the lake of fire and brimstone, where the beast and the false prophet are also; and they will be tormented day and night forever and ever* (Rev. 7:20–10, emphasis added).

## Summary

God permitted evil to defeat evil. God created only good creatures and permitted evil which is the best way possible to achieve the best of all possible worlds. The End is not the best world *conceivable*, but it is the best world *achievable*, given the fee choices of human beings and angels. God's defeat of all evil is gradual but complete through all history, and points to the glory of God. Sin and evil was *officially* defeated on the Cross, is *practically* being defeated as believers are sanctified and will *actually* be defeated upon Christ's return. Paul says, the wisdom which none of the rulers of this age has understood; for if they had understood it they would not have crucified the Lord of glory" (1 Cor. 2:8).

### Questions to Answer
1) How does the very nature of God help us understand that ultimately evil will be defeated?
2) Explain the different conditions in which God has tested and judged sinful humans.

3) Explain how the different books of the Bible unfold the gradual plan of God to defeat evil?

4) How is sin to be defeated in the believer's life through the work of Christ?

5) How did Christ defeat evil by his death on the cross, resurrection and return to earth?

# Appendix A:

# When Does Human Life Begin?

There are scientific, biblical and social evidence that a human soul (life) is present at the moment of conception. Modern fetology has brought to light amazing insights into the growth of this tiny person in her mother's womb. The following is a vivid witness to the full humanness or personhood of the prenatal child.

### Scientific Evidence that Human Life Begins at Conception

#### First Month–Actualization
- She is conceived, all her human characteristics are present (in DNA including her sex/gender).
- She implants or "nests" in her mother's uterus (at one week).
- Her heart muscle pulsates (at three weeks).
- Her head, arms, and legs begin to appear.

**Second Month–Development**

- Her brain waves can be detected (at forty to forty–two days).
- Her nose, eyes, ears, and toes appear.
- Her heart beats and blood flows (her own type).
- Her skeleton develops.
- She has her own unique fingerprints.
- She is sensitive to touch on her lips and has reflexes.
- All her bodily systems are present and functioning.

**Third Month–Movement**

- She swallows, squints, and swims.
- She grasps with her hands and moves her tongue.
- She can even suck her thumb.
- She can feel organic pain (at eight to thirteen weeks).

**Fourth Month–Grown**

- Her weight increases 600 percent (to ½ birth weight).
- She grows up to eight to ten inches long.
- She can hear her mother's voice.

**Fifth Month–viability**

- Her skin, hair, and nails develop.
- She dreams (i.e., has rapid eye movement).
- She can cry (if air is present).
- She can live outside the womb.
- She is only halfway to her scheduled birth date.

These characteristics make the human identity of the unborn unmistakable from the moment of conception: It is a human soul (life) from its very inception.

## Biblical Evidence for the Full Humanity of the Fetus

The scriptural data and arguments pertinent to this position can be summarized as follows.

1. Unborn babies are called *children*, and this is the same Greek word used of infants and young children (Luke 1:41, 44; 2:12, 16 cf. Ex. 21:22) and sometimes even of adults (1 Kings 3:17).

2. The unborn are created by God (Ps. 139:13) just as God created Adam and Eve in His image (Gen. 1:27).

3. The life of the unborn is protected by the same punishment for injury or death (Ex. 21:22) as that of an adult (Gen. 9:6).

4. Christ was human (the God–man) from the point when He was conceived in Mary's womb (Matt. 1:20–21; Luke 1:26–27).

5. The image of God includes "male and female" (Gen. 1:27), and it is a scientific fact that maleness or femaleness (sex/gender) is determined at the moment of conception.

6. Unborn children possess personal attributes, distinctive of humans, such as sin (Ps. 51:5) and joy (Luke 1:44).

7. Personal pronouns are used to describe unborn children (Jer. 1:5; Matt. 1:20–21) just as they are of any other human being.

8. The unborn are said to be known intimately and personally by God in the same way He

would know any other person (Ps. 139:15–16; Jer. 1:5).

9.   The unborn are even called by God before birth (Gen. 25:22–23; Judg. 13:2–7; Isa 49:1, 5; Gal. 1:15).

Taken together, these scriptural points leave no doubt that unborn children are just as human—persons in God's image—as are new born babies or adults. From the very moment of conception, they are created in His likeness. Their prenatal life is precious in God's eyes, and protected by His prohibition against murder (Gen. 9:6; Ex. 20:13).

### Scripture Used to Show Life Does Not Begin at Conception

Some biblical verses are used to support the position that the unborn child is not human. The following brief responses show these conclusions are not warranted.

Genesis 2:7 says that man "became a living being" only after God gave him breath. Some argue, therefore the unborn are not human until they leave the womb.

In response, there are good reasons for not taking breath as the point of human life's beginning. First, Adam (Gen. 2:7) was a unique case as he was directly created by God. The fact that he did not become human until he breathed is not decisive for determining when naturally conceived human life begins. This is because Adam was never conceived and born like other humans, he was directly created. Second, "breath" (in Gen. 2:7) means "life." So, life began when God gave human life to Adam, not simply because he began to breathe. Third, this no more proves when individual human life begins today than does the fact that he was created as an adult proves that human life does not begin until we are adults. Finally, non–rational animals breathe but are not human (Gen. 7:21–22).

Isaiah 57:16 says "the breath of those whom I have made" seems to suggest that life is connected with God giving or withholding breath (cf. Job 34:14–15). Therefore, it is reasoned no human life exists before a baby begins to breathe.

In response, if breath is equated with the presence of human life, then the loss of breath would mean the loss of humanness. But the Bible clearly says that humans continue to exist after they stop breathing (Phil. 1:23; 2 Cor. 5:6–8). As shown above, Scripture sees human life in the womb before breathing begins (Ps. 51:5; Matt. 1:20). Medical science supports this as many who stop breathing later revived. Furthermore, these verses on breath speak not of the beginning of human life but the initial coming–out event. Birth is the human debut into the world. Breath is about the beginning of observable human life, not the beginning of an actual human life. Birth, even in biblical times, was seen as the emergence of life in the natural visible world. They even knew that the baby was alive in the womb for the mother who could feel the unborn baby move (Luke 1:44).

Ecclesiastes 6:3–5 says "the miscarriage . . . comes in futility and goes into obscurity; . . . It never sees the sun and it never knows anything." This is used to argue that the unborn are no more than the dead, who know nothing.

In response, knowledge is not necessary to humanness. The miscarried child not knowing anything does not mean she is not human. If so, then adults would not be human after they die. The same book says there is no "knowledge" in the grave (9:10). The context of these passages is simply making the point that people not in the world cannot enjoy its opportunities (Eccl. 9:9). If a lack of knowledge makes one subhuman, then the ignorant or uneducated would be less human than the educated.

## Social Evidence for the Full Humanity (Personhood) of the Unborn

There are important social arguments for protecting the human rights of unborn children. Everyone accepts that embryos have human parents. It is unreasonable to insist that a human embryo is not human. No biologist has difficulty identifying an unborn horse as a horse. Therefore, we should not be compelled to decide that an unborn human should not be considered anything but human.

Human life does not stop and then restart. It is not intermittent, it is a continuous, uninterrupted flow of human life from generation to generation, parent to child. New individual humans appear through conception. Therefore, the newly formed life is fully human as his or her parents.

Modern fetology recognizes that the same baby cared for, for example being ill and needing a diagnosis and treatment is the same before birth as after birth. Modern medical care has made it possible for premature babies to live much earlier outside the womb. Some twenty-week–old fetuses have survived. It would seem to follow, if they were human when they came out of the womb at five months, then they were human if they stayed in the womb. Therefore, there are no grounds for killing them up to nine months. It is not unreal to imagine a modern hospital in which medical staff in one room rush to save a five–month–old preemie, while in another room others murder a baby in the womb who is younger or older than five months.

Arguments in favor of abortion apply equally to infanticide and euthanasia. If unborn children can be murdered because of deformity, poverty, or undesirability, then infants and the elderly can be disposed of for the same reasons. There is no legitimate difference, they all involve the same patient, undertake the same procedure, and have the same result.

Abortion has been declared wrong by many societies throughout history, both Christian and pagan. The Code of Hammurabi (18th century B.C.) contained a penalty for unintentionally causing a miscarriage. The Mosaic Law (15th century B.C.) exacted the same penalty for injury to both unborn baby and mother. The Persian ruler Tiglath-pileser (c. 12th century B.C.) punished women who caused themselves to abort. The Greek physician Hippocrates (c. 460–377 B.C.) opposed abortion by oath. Jews and Christians opposed abortion practices in the 1st and 2nd centuries. Seneca (2nd century) praised his mother for not having him aborted. Augustine (354–430), Thomas Aquinas (1225–1274) and John Calvin (1509–1564) all considered abortion immoral. English common law exacted a punishment for taking life by abortion. American law in all 50 states prior to 1973 opposed abortion.

Discrimination against anyone's life based on circumstantial matters (such as size, age, location, or functional ability) is morally wrong. These are the actual grounds on which abortionists consider the unborn child to be non–human. On this basis, we could discriminate against pygmies because they are too small, or against ethnic minorities because of where they live, or against the handicapped and elderly because they lack certain faculties.

If we can eliminate babies from the human community because they are unwanted, there is nothing to stop the elimination of other so-called societal undesirables.

Both science and Scripture support the view that an individual human life begins at conception. There are no actual, essential differences between being human and being a human person—there are only functional differences. It is morally wrong to murder an innocent human life.

# Appendix B:

## The Evil of Racism & Slavery

The idea that there is a superior race, of whatever ethnicity, is contrary to the most fundamental teaching of Scripture. There is only one race—the human race—and we are all part of it. There are many ethnic groups, but only one race—the Adamic race, which includes all of us. Several arguments advanced for racism and slavery have misused Scripture to support them. The following is offered in response.

### RACISM

#### The Mark of Cain

Some have thought that the mark of Cain was that which designated him a race into which others were not to marry (Gen. 4:15). However, there is no such reason given anywhere in Scripture for this. It was actually a mark of protection for him, for the text says,

So the LORD said to him, "Therefore whoever kills Cain, vengeance will be taken on him sevenfold." And the LORD appointed a sign for Cain, so that no one finding him would slay him. (Gen. 4:15)

Hence this mark or sign had nothing to do with color or ethnic groups that had not even developed yet (cf. Gen. 11).

### The Command Not to Intermarry with Other Nations

There is no doubt that in the Old Testament God forbade intermarriage or condemned His people for intermarrying with those of other nations. For instance, foreign wives were part of Solomon's demise (1 Kings 11:1-3), and Ezra demanded that the Israelites divorce those they had married from among the heathen (Ezra 10:10-11, 17-19). However, in each case the reason was moral, nor racial. Ezra called the alien spouses "pagan" (vv. 17-18). When Solomon was condemned for his foreign brides, the reason was clearly stated: "You shall not [intermarry] with them, nor shall they [intermarry] with you, for they will surely turn your heart away after their gods" (1 Kings 11:2). Finally, God did sanction marriage with people of varying ethnic groups. God blessed Rahab and Ruth, both of whom were brought into the bloodline of the Messiah by intermarriage with Jews. They were women of faith (cf. Joshua 2:9-11; Ruth 1:16-17; Heb. 11:31).

### God Desired Nations to Be Separate

Some have thought that God desires all nations to be distinct, for Acts 17:26 says, "having determined their appointed times and the boundaries of their habitation." If God has so determined their identity, then it is suggested that to pass those boundaries in intermarriage is wrong. However, this kind of reasoning is misdirected for several reasons. First, the statement is descriptive, not prescriptive. It is not a prohibition against migration. Second,

the statement is general, not specific, being about nations, not individuals. If it were about individuals, then
Ruth and Rahab would have been excluded also, yet they
were included in the bloodline of the Messiah (cf. Matt.
1). Third, the text itself speaks against racism, declaring
that "He made from one man every nation of mankind
to live on all the face of the earth . . ." (Acts 17:26). Thus,
reinforcing that there are not many races, there is only
one—the human race.

### The Curse of Canaan

Probably the most misused passage of all is Genesis
9. This is where God denounced Noah's descendants
through Canaan, the son of Ham, saying, "Cursed be
Canaan; A servant of servants He shall be to his brothers."
(Gen. 9:25). However, this kind of interpretation over-
looks several important facts. First, there is nothing in the
text about a curse on black or African people. Second, the
curse has nothing to do with the color of one's skin. Third,
the descendants of Canaan were the Canaanites of the
Promised Land who were cursed by God and destroyed
by the Israelites in the book of Joshua. It has nothing to do
with those who come from or live in Africa.

### Basis for Ethnic Intermarriage

There are several strong reasons from Scripture that
God approves of ethnic intermarriage. First, all ethnic
groups are from the same race—the human race. The
New Testament specifically repeats that we are all "from
one blood" (Acts 17:26). Second, there are biblically ap-
proved cases of ethnic intermarriage (such as Ruth's and
Rahab's). Third, when Moses married an Ethiopian woman and was criticized for doing so, God intervened and
judged those who disapproved (Num. 12:1-15). Finally,
the scriptural commands applicable to marriage are to
marry "in the Lord (1 Cor. 7:39). "Do not be unequally
yoked with unbelievers" (2 Cor. 6:14) is saying, do not
marry an unbeliever.

## SLAVERY

### The Biblical Arguments Against Slavery

From the very beginning, God declared that all humans participate in the image of God (Gen. 1:27). The apostle reaffirmed this, declaring, "We are the offspring of God" (Acts 17:29), and He "has made from one blood every nation of men to dwell on all the face of the earth" (Acts 17:26). Israel, itself in slavery in Egypt, was constantly reminded by God of this (Deut. 5:15), and their emancipation became the model for the liberation of all slaves (cf. Lev. 25:40). Despite the fact that slavery was countenanced in the Semitic cultures of the day, the Mosaic law demanded that slaves eventually be set free (Ex. 21:2; Lev. 25:40). Likewise, servants had to be treated with respect (Ex. 21:20, 26).

In the New Testament, Paul declared that in Christianity "there is neither Jew nor Greek, there is neither slave nor free, there is neither male nor female; for you are all one in Christ Jesus" (Gal. 3:28). All social classes are broken down in Christ; we are all equal before God. The New Testament explicitly forbids the evil system of this world that traded in the "bodies and souls of people" (Rev. 18:13). Slave trade is so repugnant to God that He pronounces His final judgment on the evil system that perpetrated it (Rev. 17–18). Paul urges, "Servants, be obedient to those who are your masters" (Eph. 6:5; cf. Col. 3:22), he is not thereby approving of the institution of slavery, but simply alluding to the de facto situation in his day. Rather, Paul instructs them to be good employees, just as believers should be today, but he was not thereby commending slavery. Paul also instructed all believers to be obedient to de facto oppressive governments for the Lord's sake (Rom. 13:1 cf. Titus 3:1; 1 Pet. 2:13). But this in no way condones oppression and tyranny which the Bible repeatedly condemns (Ex. 2:23-25; Isa. 10:1). Law and order are necessary for peace and security (Rom. 13:2-5; 1 Pet. 2:14; 1 Tim. 2:2).

A closer look at Philemon reveals that Paul did not perpetuate slavery, but actually undermined it, for he urged Philemon, Onesimus' owner, to treat him as "a beloved brother" (v. 16). So, by emphasizing the inherent equality of all human beings, both by creation and redemption, the Bible laid down the very moral principles that were used to overthrow slavery and help restore the dignity and freedom of all persons of whatever color or ethnic group.

Slavery is unethical and unbiblical and neither Paul's actions nor his writings approve of this debasing form of treatment. In fact, it was the application of biblical principles that ultimately led to the overthrow of slavery.

# Bibliography

Anselm, *St. Anselm: Basic Writings*. 2nd ed. Open Court, 1962.

Aquinas, Thomas. *Summa Theologica.* Translated by Fathers of the English Dominican Province. Vol. 1–5. Allen, TX: Christian Classics, 1948.

_____. *On Evil*. Edited by Jean Oesterle. South Bend: University of Notre Dame Press, 1995.

Arminius, Jacob. *The Writings of James Arminius*. 3 vols. Translated by James Nichols and W. R. Bagnall. Grand Rapids, Baker, 1956.

Augustine. *City of God.* New York: Random House, 1950.

Calvin, John. *Institutes of the Christian Religion*. 2 vols. Translated by Ford Lewis Battles. Edited by John Baillie. In *Library of Christian Classics*. Vols. 20–21. Philadelphia: Westminster, 1960.

Edwards, Jonathan. *The Works of Jonathan Edwards*. Vol. 1–2. Banner of Truth, 1974.

Geisler, Norman L. & Douglas E. Potter. *A Popular Survey of Bible Doctrine*, NGIM, 2015.

_____. *What in Cremation is Going On?* Bastion Books, 2016.

_____. *A Prolegomena to Evangelical Theology*. NGIM, 2016.

_____. *The Bible: Its Origin, Nature & Collection, NGIM Guide to Bible Doctrine.* Vol. 1, NGIM, 2016.

_____. *The Doctrine of Angels & Demons, NGIM Guide to Bible Doctrine.* Vol. 5, NGIM, 2016.

_____. *The Doctrine of Christ, NGIM Guide to Bible Doctrine.* Vol. 3, NGIM, 2016.

_____. *The Doctrine of Creation, NGIM Guide to Bible Doctrine.* Vol. 4, NGIM, 2016.

_____. *The Doctrine of God, NGIM Guide to Bible Doctrine.* Vol. 2, NGIM, 2016.

Geisler, Norman L. *Chosen But Free.* 3rd ed. Minneapolis: Bethany, 2010.

_____. *Creating God in the Image of Man?* Minneapolis: Bethany House, 1997.

_____. *Christian Ethics,* 2nd ed. Grand Rapids: Baker, 2010.

_____. *Knowing the Truth About Creation.* Ann Arbor: Servant Books, 1989.

_____. *Systematic Theology.* Minneapolis: Bethany, 2011.

_____. *The Big Book of Christian Apologetics.* Baker Books, 2012

_____. *Twelve Points That Show Christianity is True.* Bastion Books, 2012.

_____. *To Understand the Bible, Look for Jesus*, Chicago: Moody, 1979.

_____. *If God Why Evil?* Minneapolis: Bethany House, 2011.

Leibniz, Gottfried. *Theodicy.* Open Court, 1998.

Lewis, C. S. *Mere Christianity.* New York: Macmillan, 1943.

_____. *The Abolition of Man.* New York: Macmillan, 1947.

_____. *The Problem of Pain. New* York: Macmillan, 1940.

Lightner, Robert P. *Sin, the Savior & Salvation. Grand Rapids, Kregel, 1996.*

Luther, Martin. *Bondage of the Will.* Translated by Henry Cole. Grand Rapids: Baker, 1976.

Radmacher, Earl. *Salvation.* Nashville: Word, 2000.

Palmer, Edwin, H. *The Five Points of Calvinism.* Grand Rapids: Baker, 1972.

Schaff, Philip. *A Select Library of the Nicene and Post–Nicene Fathers of the Christian Church.* Grand Rapids: Eerdmans, 1988–1991.

Walvoord, John, & Roy Zuck, eds. *The Bible Knowledge Commentary.* Vols. 1–2. Wheaton: Victor, 1987.

NORM GEISLER INTERNATIONAL MINISTRIES

Norm Geisler International Ministries is dedicated to carrying on the life's work of its co-founder, Norman L. Geisler. Described as a cross between Billy Graham and Thomas Aquinas, Norm Geisler, PhD, is a prolific author, professor, apologist, philosopher, and theologian. He has authored or co-authored over 100 books and co-founded 2 seminaries.

NGIM is focused on equipping others to proclaim and defend the Christian Faith by providing evangelism and apologetic training.

## More Information

Website:          http://NormGeisler.com
Training:         http://NGIM.org (Norm Geisler International Ministries)
e–Books:          http://BastionBooks.com
Email:            Dr.NormanGeisler@outlook.com
Facebook:         http://facebook.com/normgeisler
Twitter:          https://www.twitter.com/normgeisler
Videos:           http://www.youtube.com/user/DrNormanLGeisler/videos
Biblical Inerrancy:  http://DefendingInerrancy.com
Seminaries:       Southern Evangelical Seminary http://SES.edu
                  Veritas Evangelical Seminary http://VES.edu

# Other books from

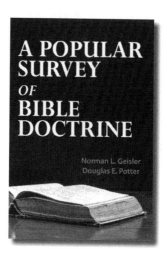

C HRISTIANS, more than ever, need a basic introduction to Bible doctrine that is systematic and true to Scripture. This book is a popular introduction to the study of Bible doctrine firmly in the evangelical tradition. Each chapter covers a biblical doctrine, stresses its doctrinal importance and inter-connectedness to formulating a Christian world view. The study questions provided help reinforce the material and make it usable even for a formal study of Bible doctrine. It is ideal for personal study and in groups for the home, church, school or ministry environment.

www.NGIM.org

**Guide to
Bible Doctrine**

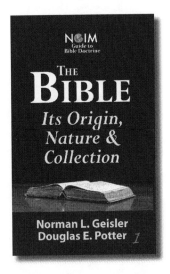

**NGIM Guide to Bible Doctrine Book 1**

This is a popular introduction to the study of the doctrine of the Bible firmly rooted in the evangelical tradition. Each chapter covers an area of the doctrine of the Bible, stresses its basis, doctrinal importance and interconnectedness to formulating a Christian view of the Bible and other doctrines. The study questions provided help reinforce the material and make it usable even for a formal study of the Bible's nature. It is ideal for personal study or in groups for the home, church, school or ministry environment.

**www.NGIM.org**

### Guide to
### Bible Doctrine

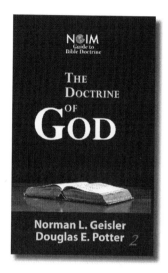

## NGIM GUIDE TO BIBLE DOCTRINE BOOK 2

THIS is a popular introduction to the study of the biblical doctrine of God firmly in the evangelical tradition. Each chapter covers an area of the doctrine of God, stresses its biblical basis, doctrinal importance and interconnectedness to formulating a Christian view of God. The study questions provided help reinforce the material and make it usable even for a formal study of God's nature. It is ideal for personal study or in groups for the home, church, school or ministry environment.

www.NGIM.org